THE PUGLIAN COOKBOOK

The Puglian *Cookbook*

BRINGING THE FLAVORS OF PUGLIA HOME

Viktorija Todorovska

A SURREY BOOK

AGATE

CHICAGO

Printed in China.

All photographs except the photo on page 47 copyright © Michael Potts.
The photo on page 47 is copyright © iStockphoto.
Design by Brandtner Design.

Library of Congress Cataloging-in-Publication Data

Todorovska, Viktorija, 1971-
  The Puglian cookbook : bringing the flavors of Puglia home / Viktorija Todorovska.
      p. cm.
  Includes index.
    Summary: "Recipes from the Puglian region of southern Italy, with photographs"--Provided by the publisher.
  ISBN-13: 978-1-57284-117-8 (pbk.)
  ISBN-10: 1-57284-117-6 (paperback)
1. Cooking, Italian--Southern style. 2. Cooking--Italy--Puglia. 3. Cookbooks. I. Title.
  TX723.2.S65T63 2011
  641.5945'75--dc22
                    2010047985

11 12 13 14   10 9 8 7 6 5 4 3 2 1

Surrey Books is an imprint of Agate Publishing. Agate books are available in bulk at discount prices.
For more information, go to agatepublishing.com.

Acknowledgments

THIS BOOK WOULD NOT HAVE BEEN POSSIBLE WITHOUT MY MANY FRIENDS, BOTH in Chicago and in Puglia. First of all, I want to thank Tom Valenti and Paola Pinto for introducing me to some wonderful Puglian cooks who shared with me the recipes of their tradition and helped me get to know their region. Paola's coordination made the research for this book manageable, and the recipes she shared with me have a special place in my cooking and teaching.

I also want to thank all of my friends in the United States who believed in this project and supported me through the writing and dreaming. They selflessly taste-tested the recipes and provided invaluable feedback. Special thanks go to Michelle Chaisson, who not only served as a research assistant on a trip to Puglia but also tasted many of the recipes (including some that required an adventurous spirit) and helped with some of the photography. This book would not have been the same without her support and help. Rissa Reddan, who was always up for a taste test, constantly brainstormed ideas with me and believed in the project. Brooke Vuckovic provided much-appreciated guidance, read the first draft of the book, tested recipes, and gave invaluable feedback.

My greatest thanks go to my husband, Michael Potts, who enthusiastically supported the project from day one and even before. His energy and enthusiasm never wavered through multiple trips to Puglia; many days, nights, and weekends of cooking; and many days of photo shoots. He fearlessly tasted every recipe in the book and provided constructive feedback. This book would truly not have been possible without him.

Thanks also go to the people of Puglia, who are proud of their region and its traditions. They always welcome me with open arms, helping me discover the beauties and secrets of this amazing piece of land, one recipe at a time.

Finally, thanks to Agate Publishing and Doug Seibold for believing in this book and my mission to share my easy and delicious Puglian recipes with food lovers everywhere.

Any mistakes in the book are, of course, mine and mine alone.

Table of Contents

GALLIPOLI

LECCE

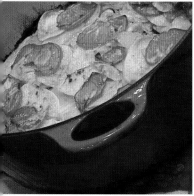

Introduction

"Puglia is…Puglia," says Francesco with a twinkle in his eyes. He's not able to put into words his feelings about this beautiful region—the place where he has spent half of his life, and to which he still regularly returns.

Indeed, Puglia is difficult to describe. It is the impossibly blue sky, the centuries-old gnarled olive trees, the red iron-rich soil, and the bright sun of the Italian south. It is also the crusty bread

of Altamura; the bitter chicory that is the backbone of so many Puglian dishes; the sweet ripe tomatoes that make all other tomatoes pale in comparison; and the rich, almost purple, Primitivo wine that tastes like pure sunshine. It is also the warmth of the Puglian people, the openness with which they welcome you into their shops and homes, and the emotion with which they talk about the region that has been their home for centuries.

The traditional foods of Puglia have what food-and-wine writer Matt Kramer calls "transparency of flavors." The ingredients shine unadulterated, combined into simple dishes free of elaborate sauces. The flavors are simple yet enchanting; the dishes are uncomplicated and unpretentious. They tell the history of a region that has been conquered by many but has always remained true to itself. Puglian cuisine is peasant food, relying on locally and seasonally available ingredients. This peasant character is evident in the omission or less frequent use of certain ingredients: meat—mostly lamb—is used sparingly and mostly in dishes for special occasions, such as celebrations and Sunday dinners. No eggs are used in the preparation of the

fresh pasta. Fresh vegetables, legumes, and olive oil are the cornerstones of this culinary tradition, which is full of imagination, art, and love.

Puglia is a large region, and its cooking varies greatly between its 800-mile (1300-km) coastline and the plains and mountains of its interior. No single cookbook can do justice to this diversity. I have gathered a set of representative recipes from the region that showcases the principles on which the cuisine is based: simplicity, integrity of ingredients, and flavors.

For those who might feel a little intimidated about taking on recipes from an unfamiliar part of the world—relax! I am not a restaurant chef. The dishes here might be found on menus in small villages all over Puglia, but the recipes are intended to be easily prepared at home. I tested every recipe in my own kitchen

using ingredients that are readily available in U.S. supermarkets
and equipment that is common
to most kitchens. The techniques
I've used to prepare these recipes
are simple and explained in detail,
so beginners will be able to follow
them without trouble.

You can also rest assured that
every recipe has been tested by
the cooking enthusiasts who at-
tend my cooking classes and by my friends as well. All the photos in the book are
of the actual dishes we have prepared and consumed. No chemicals or food-styling
instruments were used to modify the appearance of the dishes, so the pictures rep-
resent what your dishes will actually look like.

This cookbook reflects the beauty and spirit of Puglia—the most delicious foods
are the simplest. There are no long lists of ingredients, no special equipment or
techniques are involved, and no advanced culinary skills are required. Some of the
dishes in this cookbook are so simple that they can only be appreciated when you
taste them. I hope you will enjoy many of them as you embrace new culinary traditions from this special corner of Italy.

Viktorija Todorovska
Chicago, Illinois

Ingredients

FOLLOWING IS A PARTIAL LIST OF THE INGREDIENTS MOST FREQUENTLY USED IN this book. After each primary ingredient, I've described its use in Puglian cuisine in general as well as in the recipes that follow.

ANCHOVIES

Many of the recipes in this book call for anchovies, an ingredient commonly used in Puglia to add depth of flavor to a dish. The anchovies melt in warm olive oil, and their initial flavor is not noticeable in the final dish—the only thing that lingers is a rich, mild saltiness.

When I first started using anchovies in my cooking, my friends were suspicious. Some had unpleasant memories of whole anchovies on pizza. But the anchovies in these recipes are used only to flavor the dishes. The flavor is so gentle that even some of my vegetarian friends don't mind having their food seasoned with them. I use salt-cured anchovies, which you can find in fine grocery stores and Italian groceries. Canned anchovies work well, too.

Of course, you can always omit anchovies from a recipe, but doing so will change the flavor of the dish slightly. If you decide to omit the anchovies, add a little more extra virgin olive oil to boost the flavor.

CANNED TOMATOES

Puglia grows some of the most flavorful tomatoes I have ever had. From the tiny, dark-red grape tomatoes often dried and preserved for the winter to the large, almost apple-sized, juicy tomatoes, Puglian tomatoes have an unforgettable flavor that is difficult to find other places. Since tomatoes of that quality and ripeness are difficult to find outside Puglia, I have opted to use canned tomatoes in many of the recipes. High-quality canned tomatoes are canned at their peak and, as a result, are fully ripe and sweet, preserving the flavor of a real tomato ripened under the southern Italian sun. The most widely available high-quality canned tomatoes in the

United States are the ones that come from San Marzano (which is always identified on the can). They are dark red, sweet, and full flavored.

GARLIC

As a general rule, American cooks who prepare Italian food use more garlic than their Italian counterparts. In Italy, whole cloves of garlic might be used to impart aroma and flavor while a dish is cooking, but they are often removed before serving. The amounts of garlic recommended in the recipes in this book follow a middle-of-the-road approach: probably a little more than an Italian grandmother would use, but a little less than someone cooking in an Italian restaurant in the United States would. So, when using garlic, go with what you like best. If you like it, serve the dishes with the garlic, or use whole cloves of garlic while cooking and discard them before the dish is served. But remember—garlic is a key flavoring ingredient, so do not exclude it completely.

To prevent garlic from burning, never add onions and garlic at the same time. Onions always need to cook for a while before they soften. Garlic cooks much faster and will burn by the time the onions start to soften. Burnt garlic tastes bitter and will ruin a dish.

If a recipe calls for garlic alone, add it to the olive oil when you pour the olive oil in the pan and let it warm up as the oil does. Throwing garlic into hot olive oil will cause it to instantly burn around the edges.

Also, you should never cook garlic until it is brown. At that point, it is burnt and should be discarded (especially since it is likely to continue cooking when you add the rest of the ingredients). As soon as garlic starts to change color, it is cooked.

OLIVE OIL

People often ask me if you can cook with extra virgin olive oil. Not only *can* you, but you *should!* Use extra virgin olive oil whenever possible, as it is one of the healthiest fats. I do not use any other oil—even for baking. Some extra virgin olive oils are quite pricey, but plenty are good and reasonably priced.

Make sure to buy oil frequently, as it goes rancid pretty quickly. Keep your olive oil in a dark and cool place and use it within a year or so of its date of harvest (which should be printed on the bottle or can).

When cooking with olive oil, remember that it burns faster than other oils, so make sure not to overheat it. If the oil starts smoking, it is burnt and should not be used (for health and flavor reasons). Discard any oil that has started smoking and start fresh.

RED PEPPER

Southern Italians often use red pepper, either whole or crushed, but only in moderation: Their dishes are rarely extra spicy. Just as with everything else, the use of pepper is a matter of balance. I like spicy foods, so I tend to add a little more red pepper to my food than I've specified in my recipes. If you want to do so as well, go ahead, but know that in Puglia, dishes are rarely hot and spicy.

GREENS

Puglians eat a lot of chicory, a dark and slightly bitter green. Fresh chicory is difficult to find in the United States, but dandelion greens are an excellent substitute. If you prefer a different green, feel free to experiment, but keep in mind that cooking times and flavors will vary.

PECORINO CHEESE

Pecorino is a sheep's milk cheese (*pecora* means sheep in Italian), and it is made in several Italian regions, most famously in Lazio, around Rome (*pecorino Romano*) and in Sardinia (*pecorino Sardo*). Depending on where it comes from, pecorino cheese will have a slightly different flavor, but the important thing is to use aged

pecorino cheese, which is a hard, granular, grating cheese. It is quite salty and has a robust, nutty flavor that intensifies with age.

SEMOLINA FLOUR

Most southern Italian pasta is made from a hard wheat flour called semolina or durum wheat flour in the United States. It has a yellowish cast and is coarser than all-purpose flour. Some brands are too coarse and require more work when making pasta. Look for a finer-ground version in an Italian grocery or health food store. If you can only find coarse-ground flour (which can look more like polenta than flour), mix it with a little all-purpose flour to make the kneading easier.

Things Worth Making from Scratch

FOR ME, EATING WELL IS WORTH THE EFFORT. EATING WELL MEANS CHOOSING the freshest ingredients and preparing those ingredients in a way that makes them shine. It takes some effort to make things yourself, but the reward is well worth it—not only for the flavor but also because making things from scratch changes your relationship with food.

FRESH PASTA

Fresh pasta is one of the most delicious indulgences. It is so simple and yet so delicious that I am always surprised people do not make it more often. The students in my cooking classes are invariably amazed by how easy and fun it is to make fresh pasta.

Once you make your own pasta and taste the difference, you'll dream about it and make it every chance you get. Even my friends' kids ask to make fresh pasta every time they come over. Making fresh pasta is a fun activity—a way for a family to cook and enjoy time together. It helps people come together around food, and the results are so delicious that the experience becomes unforgettable.

The most common shapes of fresh pasta in Puglia—orecchiette and cavatelli—do not require pasta machines, just a little bit of time and love for good food. They are also fun for both kids and adults and, because they are somewhat unusual, making them always feels like a learning experience.

You'll find my recipe for making cavatelli on page 61.

OLIO SANTO

This brilliant condiment, olive oil made hot with the addition of dried red peppers (or crushed red pepper), is a staple on every table in southern Puglia. After several days, the olive oil absorbs the flavor of the peppers and becomes very spicy. It is the perfect condiment for such Puglian dishes as potatoes, beans and greens, and roasted green peppers. It's also delicious with simple, fresh bread and good cheese.

To make olio santo, combine 1 part dried peppers or pepper flakes and 4 parts good olive oil in a clean jar. Let it sit for several days in a cool, dark spot. Use judiciously.

Olive oil purists object to flavored olive oils, but I find this combination better than the sum of its parts. It is true that the flavor of the olive oil itself does not come through quite as strongly, but drizzled over a simple Puglian dish, this oil shines.

BREADCRUMBS

Most people never even consider making breadcrumbs from scratch. But once you have had pasta or a casserole with fresh, homemade breadcrumbs, nothing else will do. Homemade breadcrumbs actually taste like the toasted bread they are made from, so they enhance a dish's flavor. Also, because they tend to be less regular in shape and size than the commercial product, they add an interesting texture component.

To make your own breadcrumbs, use good-quality crusty bread. I use Pugliese, a big loaf of white Italian bread with a wonderful crust. If this is not an option, you may use any good baguette. Of course, choose a flavorful bread, or your breadcrumbs will be as boring as the bread they came from.

To prepare the breadcrumbs, slice the bread and place the slices on a baking sheet. Toast the bread in the oven at a low temperature (250°F [120°C]) for an hour or so, turning each slice over halfway through. When the bread feels sufficiently crunchy, take it out of the oven, let it cool, and put in the food processor. I prefer to include the crust when making my breadcrumbs, but you can remove the crust and process only the middle, if you prefer.

Appetizers

Puglian appetizers spotlight the star ingredients of the region: olives, greens, olive oil, and ripe tomatoes. They are simple, light, and flavorful. In Puglia, the dishes listed under Appetizers in this book are often served as a snack or part of a summer lunch consisting of many small plates, served at room temperature. Feel free to combine some of these recipes to make a great make-ahead brunch or lunch or a tasty party spread.

Tomato Bruschetta
See recipe on page 46

Beans and Greens

This dish is a cornerstone of Puglian cuisine, especially in southern Puglia. It combines some of the most common Puglian ingredients: beans, greens, and olive oil. It is also the perfect illustration of two of the unique features of Puglian cuisine: It is easy to make yet full of flavor and deeply satisfying. Accompanied by some inky Primitivo or a good Puglian rosé, it makes a perfect summer dinner. I also often serve it as an appetizer to kick off a dinner party. It tastes great even at room temperature and requires so little effort that you can enjoy your guests and still serve something they are sure to love. In Puglia, the beans of choice are fava and the greens are chicory. I use chickpeas and dandelion greens, a close relative of chicory, which are much easier to find in the United States. Dandelion greens have a pleasant bitterness and lots of flavor.

YIELD: 8 SERVINGS

For the bean spread:

> 2 cups (273 mL) dried chickpeas
>
> 1 large yellow onion, cut into quarters
>
> 1 large carrot, peeled and cut into 1-inch (2.5-cm) pieces
>
> 3 cloves garlic, whole
>
> 2 teaspoons (10 mL) sea salt, plus more, to taste

1. Soak the beans overnight in cold water.

2. Drain the beans and put them in a large pot. Add water to cover the beans by about 2 inches (5 cm). Add the onion, carrot, garlic, and about 2 teaspoons (10 mL) salt, and bring to a boil.

3. Reduce the heat to low and cook slowly for about 3 hours, until the beans are soft and can be mashed with a wooden spoon.

4. Drain, reserving 1 cup (236 mL) of the cooking liquid. When the beans are cool enough to handle, remove the onion and carrot.

5. Put the beans and garlic in a food processor and pulse until the purée reaches a uniform consistency. If the purée is too dry, gradually add a little of the cooking water. Add salt to taste.

For the greens:

> 2 bunches dandelion greens, washed and cut into bite-sized pieces
>
> Salt, to taste
>
> Olive oil, for drizzling
>
> Toasted French bread or fresh vegetables (such as celery, carrots, and bell peppers), for serving

1. In a medium pot, bring 2 quarts (1.9 L) of water to a boil. Add the greens and salt and cook for 2 to 3 minutes, until the greens are wilted. Drain immediately.

2. Serve the beans surrounded by the greens. Drizzle the dish with the olive oil, and use toasted rounds of French bread or fresh vegetables to scoop the spread.

Asparagus Tart

This tart (see photo next spread) is perfect to make in the spring, even early in the season, when asparagus is just about the only fresh green vegetable at the farmer's market. It is satisfying and wows vegetarians and carnivores alike. Whether you make it for a weekend brunch or for a light dinner, the tart goes well with a simple Tomato Salad (see recipe on page 138) and a crisp Puglian rosé.

YIELD: 4 SERVINGS

½ bunch asparagus

1 frozen (9-inch [22.5-cm]) single-crust pie shell, thawed

½ cup (118 mL) grated pecorino cheese

4 eggs, lightly beaten

Salt, to taste

Freshly ground black pepper, to taste

1. Preheat the oven to 400°F (200°C).

2. Wash the asparagus and cut off the tough lower part of the stems. Boil the asparagus for 2 minutes, drain, and immediately rinse with cold water. Cut into bite-sized pieces and layer the pieces into the pie shell.

3. Sprinkle the tart with the pecorino cheese.

4. In a bowl, beat the eggs and season them with salt and pepper. Pour the eggs over the asparagus and cheese and fold the walls of the pie shell over the egg mixture.

5. Bake for 35 to 40 minutes.

Greens Tart

The escarole in this tart almost always surprises my dinner guests, as they are not familiar with this delicious and very nutritious green. It gives the tart a depth of flavor people seldom expect from a green. The tart pairs perfectly with a light- to medium-bodied red wine, such as Puglia's Salice Salentino.

Yield: 8 servings

2 tablespoons (30 mL) extra virgin olive oil, plus more for brushing the pie shells

1 large red onion, quartered and thinly sliced

1 head escarole, washed and cut into bite-sized pieces

¾ cup (177 mL) half-and-half

3 eggs, lightly beaten

1 cup (236 mL) grated pecorino cheese, divided

Salt, to taste

Freshly ground black pepper, to taste

2 frozen (9-inch [22.5-cm]) single-crust pie shells, thawed

1. Preheat the oven to 375°F (190°C).

2. In a skillet, heat the olive oil over medium heat. Add the onion and cook until soft and translucent.

3. Meanwhile, bring a pot of salted water to a boil. Add the escarole and cook for 2 minutes, or until it wilts. Drain, add to the onion, and cook for an additional 2 minutes. Remove the skillet from the heat and add the half-and-half. Let the mixture cool.

4. Add the eggs and ¾ cup (177 mL) of the pecorino cheese. Add the salt and pepper. Stir to combine the ingredients. Divide the mixture equally between the two pie shells, brush the edges of the crust with extra virgin olive oil, and bake for 40 minutes.

5. Sprinkle the remaining ¼ cup (59 mL) pecorino cheese on top of the pies and broil them for 2 minutes, or until the cheese is melted and the tops are browned.

6. Serve hot or at room temperature.

Asparagus Tart · PAGE 28

Puglian Flatbread (Puddica)

This simple Puglian flatbread is easy to make with pizza dough and delicious as a light lunch with some cheese or as a snack. You can add other toppings—olives, capers, prosciutto—but tomatoes are the most traditionally Puglian.

YIELD: 8 SERVINGS

> 1 batch (about 1½ pounds [680 g]) pizza dough
>
> 10 grape tomatoes, halved
>
> Salt, to taste
>
> Extra virgin olive oil, for brushing the dough

1. Preheat the oven to 400°F (200°C). Thoroughly oil a baking sheet.

2. Roll out the pizza dough and spread it on the prepared baking sheet. Distribute the tomatoes on top of the pizza dough, sprinkle with salt, and brush with olive oil.

3. Bake for at least 35 minutes, or until golden brown.

Note: The flatbread will keep for a couple of days in an airtight container.

Focaccia from Bari

This recipe was given to me by Graziana, a native of the port city of Bari. When she moved away from Bari, Graziana could not find any good focaccia, so she and her sister created this easy, no-fail recipe.

After learning how to make this focaccia at Graziana's house and tasting it, I too am convinced that it's the best focaccia in southern Puglia. It stands up to the best focaccia I have tasted in my travels to Bari.

YIELD: 8 SERVINGS

2¼ cups (500 g) all-purpose flour*

1 (0.25-ounce [7-g]) package active dry yeast

2 teaspoons (10 mL) sugar

2 teaspoons (10 mL) salt

2 cups (473 mL) warm water (105°–110°F [40°–43°C])

½ cup (118 mL) extra virgin olive oil

1 (14-ounce [392-g]) can whole tomatoes

2 teaspoons (10 mL) dried oregano

2 tablespoons (30 mL) capers

½ cup (118 mL) green or black olives (optional, but highly recommended)

Sea salt, to taste

1. In a large bowl, combine the flour, yeast, sugar, and salt and mix well. Slowly add the water and mix with your hands, breaking up any lumps. When the dough is smooth (it should be almost runny), cover it with a towel, wrap the bowl in a warm blanket, and let the dough rise in a warm spot for at least 1½ hours. The dough should double in size and have bubbles at the end of the rising. If you want a thicker focaccia, let the dough rise for an additional ½ hour.

* For a crunchier focaccia, use 1¾ cup (400 g) all-purpose flour and ½ cup (100 g) semolina (durum wheat) flour.

2. Meanwhile, preheat the oven to 400°F (200°C). Generously brush the bottom and sides of a large baking pan with olive oil, leaving no dry spots.

3. Spoon the focaccia dough into the pan and spread evenly. Spread the canned tomatoes on the surface of the dough and sprinkle with oregano and capers (and olives, if desired). Sprinkle with sea salt and drizzle with a little olive oil.

4. Bake for 45 minutes.

White Focaccia with Olives

Once you try this easy and delicious focaccia with no tomatoes, you will be tempted to eat it instead of bread all the time. It enhances any meal and is also great for a quick picnic-style lunch with some sliced mozzarella cheese and salami and other favorites, such as sweet and sour peppers or artichoke hearts.

YIELD: 8 SERVINGS

2¼ cups (500 g) all-purpose flour*

1 (0.25-ounce [7 g]) package active dry yeast

2 teaspoons (10 mL) sugar

2 teaspoons (10 mL) salt

2 cups (473 mL) warm water (105°–110°F [40°–43°C])

½ cup (118 mL) extra virgin olive oil

Sea salt, to taste

1 cup (236 mL) black olives, halved

1. In a large bowl, combine the flour, yeast, sugar, and salt and mix well. Slowly add the water and mix with your hands, breaking up any lumps. When the dough is smooth (it should be almost runny), cover it with a towel, wrap the bowl in a warm blanket, and let the dough rise in a warm spot for at least 1½ hours. The dough should double in size and have bubbles at the end of the rising. If you want a thicker focaccia, let the dough rise for an additional ½ hour.

2. Meanwhile, preheat the oven to 400°F (200°C). Generously brush the bottom and sides of a large baking pan with olive oil, leaving no dry spots.

3. Spoon the focaccia dough into the pan and spread evenly. Sprinkle with sea salt and distribute the olives on top of the focaccia.

4. Bake for 45 minutes.

* For a crunchier focaccia, use 1¾ cup (400 g) all-purpose flour and ½ cup (100 g) semolina (durum wheat) flour.

Pizza with Ricotta and Salami

This dish is richer than most typical Puglian dishes. In Puglia, it is served on special occasions, such as holidays or Sunday lunches. It is quick to make yet very satisfying. It pairs perfectly with Salice Salentino or another medium- to full-bodied wine. Cut into small pieces, it makes an excellent appetizer. Paired with a green salad, it makes a delicious dinner. Get the freshest, highest-quality ricotta you can find, preferably hand-dipped, as the flavor of the ricotta shines through.

YIELD: 4 SERVINGS

1 batch (about 1½ pounds [680 g]) pizza dough, divided in half

14 ounces (392 g) fresh ricotta

5 ounces (140 g) mozzarella cheese, cubed

3 ounces (84 g) salami, chopped

½ cup (118 mL) grated Parmesan cheese

2 eggs

1½ teaspoons (7.5 mL) salt

Freshly ground black pepper, to taste

1 teaspoon (5 mL) crushed red pepper (optional)

Extra virgin olive oil, for brushing

1. Preheat the oven to 400°F (200°C). Thoroughly oil a baking sheet.

2. Roll out each portion of pizza dough into a round about ¼ inch (0.5 cm) thick.

3. In a large bowl, combine the ricotta, mozzarella cheese, salami, Parmesan cheese, eggs, salt, black pepper, and red pepper (if using). Stir until the ingredients are combined and the mixture is uniform.

4. Place one of the rounds of pizza dough onto the baking sheet. Spread the cheese and salami mixture over the dough, leaving about a ½-inch (1-cm) border. Cover with the second round of dough and pinch around the edges to seal the pizza. Brush the top with olive oil and bake for about 35 minutes, or until the top of the pizza is golden brown.

Pizza with Greens

As made in Puglia, this simple and delicious appetizer features the slightly bitter chicory ubiquitous in the region. Dandelion greens, a close relative of chicory, are much easier to find in the United States and approximate the flavor of chicory. The simplicity of the dish belies its flavor. The pine nuts add a depth of flavor that allows this dish to pair well with medium-bodied wines such as Primitivo and Negroamaro.

Yield: 8 servings

> 1 package (about 1½ pounds [680 g]) pizza dough (at room temperature), divided in half*
>
> 2 bunches dandelion greens, washed and cut into bite-sized pieces
>
> 3 tablespoons (45 mL) extra virgin olive oil, plus more for brushing the dough
>
> 2 cloves garlic, peeled and thinly sliced
>
> 2 tablespoons (30 mL) pine nuts, lightly toasted

1. Preheat the oven to 400°F (200°C). Thoroughly oil a baking sheet.

2. Roll out each half of the pizza dough into a round about ¼ inch (0.5 cm) thick.

3. Boil the dandelion greens in salted water for 3 minutes, until they begin to soften. Drain. While the greens boil, heat the olive oil and garlic over medium heat. Add the drained greens and the pine nuts, toss, and cook for 3 more minutes. Set aside.

4. Place one round of dough on the oiled baking sheet. Spread the sautéed greens over the dough, leaving a ½-inch (1-cm) border around the edge. Brush the border with water. Cover the greens with the other rolled-out round of pizza dough, making sure the two circles of dough overlap. Go around the edges of the pizza and pinch the dough to seal the layers together.

5. Brush the top of the pizza generously with olive oil and bake for 20 minutes, or until the top and bottom crusts start to brown.

* You can buy refrigerated pizza dough at your neighborhood pizza place or at the grocery store. If you prefer, of course, you can always make your own.

Olio Santo

This brilliant invention is a staple on every table in the Salento peninsula in the southern part of Puglia. Olio Santo (see photo on pages 22–23) is a spicy-hot olive oil made by adding dried red peppers (or crushed red pepper). After several days, the olive oil absorbs the flavor of the peppers and becomes very spicy. It is a perfect condiment for Puglian dishes such as Puglian potatoes, beans and greens, or oven-roasted green peppers, or even simple fresh bread and some good cheese.

Olive-oil purists object to flavored olive oils, but I find this combination better than the sum of its parts. It is true that the flavor of the olive oil does not come through quite as purely as it might otherwise, but drizzled over a simple Puglian dish, this oil shines.

> **1 part dried red peppers or crushed red pepper flakes**
>
> **4 parts good olive oil**

1. Combine the peppers or pepper flakes and olive oil. Let sit for several days in a cool, dark spot. Use judiciously.

Zucchini Frittata

Zucchini Frittata (see photo next spread) is a modified version of my friend Paola's frittata. It is light and flavorful, making it a perfect summer lunch or a yummy appetizer. My guests always want to know what makes this frittata so complex and flavorful. The bread gives the frittata a fluffy texture, the milk helps it stay moist, and the pecorino cheese gives it a unique nutty sweetness. Pair it with a Puglian rosé or a crisp white wine.

YIELD: 6 SERVINGS

> 5 tablespoons (75 mL) extra virgin olive oil, divided
>
> 3 medium zucchini, halved lengthwise and thinly sliced
>
> 1 medium onion, peeled and chopped
>
> 1 thick slice crusty bread (such as Pugliese), soaked in 1 cup (236 mL) milk for 5 minutes
>
> 6 large eggs
>
> ½ cup (118 mL) grated pecorino cheese
>
> 1 teaspoon (5 mL) salt

1. Preheat the oven to 400°F (200°C).

2. In a medium pan, heat 2 tablespoons (30 mL) of the olive oil. Add the zucchini and onion and cook until they are soft, about 7 to 8 minutes. Set aside.

3. Meanwhile, break up the bread into small pieces with your hands. Reserve the milk it was soaking in.

4. In a large bowl, combine the zucchini and onion mixture, the bread and milk, the eggs, the pecorino cheese, and the salt. Stir to combine. The mixture should be quite liquid (slightly thicker than milk), If necessary, add more milk.

5. Pour the remaining olive oil (about 3 tablespoons [45 mL]) into a large pan and swirl it around to make sure the bottom and sides of the pan are well oiled. Pour the egg mixture into the pan and cook for about 15 minutes, or until the eggs are set. Brown the frittata under the broiler for a couple of minutes.

6. Serve hot or at room temperature.

Zucchini Frittata · PAGE 41

Potato Frittata

This is the perfect light lunch or dinner, especially for vegetarians. It can be served with my Tomato Salad (see recipe on page 138) and some crusty bread. It also makes a great appetizer. In Italy, frittata is served as an appetizer at room temperature, so making it ahead of time will allow you to enjoy the company of your guests. Pair with a Puglian rosé or a light- to medium-bodied red.

YIELD: 4 SERVINGS

> 3 medium Yukon Gold potatoes, peeled and cubed
>
> 5 tablespoons (75 mL) extra virgin olive oil, divided
>
> 1 medium onion, peeled and chopped
>
> ½ cup (118 mL) grated pecorino cheese
>
> ½ cup (118 mL) chopped parsley
>
> 6 large eggs
>
> 6–10 tablespoons (90–150 mL) milk
>
> Salt, to taste
>
> Freshly ground black pepper, to taste

1. Preheat the oven to 400°F (200°C).

2. Boil the potatoes in salted water until done (a fork should go through the potato cubes with little effort). Drain the potatoes and set aside.

3. In a pan, heat 2 tablespoons (30 mL) of the olive oil. Add the onion and cook until it is soft and translucent.

4. In a large bowl, combine the cooked potatoes, cooked onions, pecorino cheese, and parsley.

5. In a separate bowl, beat together the eggs and milk for about 30 seconds, or until combined. Add the egg and milk mixture to the potato mixture and stir to combine. The mixture should be quite liquid. If it is thick, add more milk. Season with the salt and pepper.

6. Pour the remaining olive oil in a large, oven-safe pan and swirl it around to cover the bottom and sides. Pour the egg mixture into the pan and cook in the oven for 15 minutes, or until the eggs are set. Brown the frittata under the broiler for a couple of minutes.

7. Serve hot or at room temperature.

Summer Frittata

This frittata has all the flavors of summer and makes a perfect lunch or light dinner when ripe tomatoes are in season. Grape or cherry tomatoes are usually easier to find year round, so I recommend using those. Regular tomatoes are great too, when they are perfectly ripe and flavorful.

This frittata pairs well with a Puglian rosé or a lighter red wine.

Yield: 4 servings

>   1 thick slice crusty white bread, soaked in 1 cup (236 mL) milk for 5 minutes
>   6 large eggs
>   1 cup (236 mL) grated pecorino cheese
>   1 teaspoon (5 mL) salt
>   1 teaspoon (5 mL) freshly ground black pepper
>   3 tablespoons (45 mL) extra virgin olive oil
>   4 ounces (112 g) mozzarella cheese, chopped
>   1 pint (473 mL) grape (or cherry) tomatoes, chopped
>   3 ounces (84 g) arugula

1. Preheat the oven to 400°F (200°C).

2. Break up the bread into small pieces with your hands. Reserve the milk it was soaking in.

3. In a bowl, mix together the eggs, pecorino cheese, bread, and milk. Stir to combine. Add the salt and pepper.

4. In a large, oven-safe pan, heat the olive oil and swirl it around to cover the entire bottom of the pan and about 1 inch (2.5 cm) up the sides. Pour in the egg mixture and cook for 2 minutes, or until the eggs start to set around the rim. Transfer the pan to the oven and continue cooking for 12 to 15 minutes, or until the eggs are completely set and a golden crust starts to form on top.

5. When the frittata is cooked, sprinkle with the mozzarella cheese, tomatoes, and arugula and let rest for about 2 minutes.

6. Serve hot or at room temperature.

Tomato Bruschetta

There are multiple recipes for tomato-based bruschetta topping (see photo on page 24–25). This is my interpretation, and in the summer it graces my dinner table almost every day. It has won more compliments than any other appetizer I make, and even guests who do not like tomatoes cannot stop eating it. Now that is a good recipe!

YIELD: 4–8 SERVINGS

16 ounces (454 g) ripe tomatoes, chopped*

½ red onion, finely chopped

1½ teaspoons (7.5 mL) sea salt

3 tablespoons (45 mL) extra virgin olive oil

1½ tablespoons (22.5 mL) red wine vinegar

4 thick slices crusty white bread, halved (or 8 smaller slices) and toasted

1 tablespoon (15 mL) chopped basil

1. Combine the tomatoes and onion and season with the salt, olive oil, and vinegar.

2. Spoon this mixture onto the toasted bread, sprinkle with the basil, and serve.

* In the summer and fall, buy the freshest and ripest tomatoes you can find. In the winter, buy grape or cherry tomatoes, as they will have more flavor than larger tomatoes.

Soups

Puglian soups are often thick and contain beans, an affordable way to add protein to the diet in times when meat was not as affordable. These soups grew out of the *cucina povera* (peasant cuisine) tradition and often combine ingredients in creative ways to create rich, satisfying meals.

White Bean and Escarole Soup
See recipe on the next spread

White Bean Soup

White beans are a very popular legume in Puglia, where they add substance to people's diets in the winter. They are often used in pasta dishes and soups. This simple white bean soup is perfect for cool days and pairs well with White Focaccia with Olives (see recipe on page 36).

Y<small>IELD:</small> 6 <small>SERVINGS</small>

2 tablespoons (30 mL) extra virgin olive oil

2 medium onions, peeled and finely chopped

2 cloves garlic, peeled and thinly sliced

10–15 ripe grape (or cherry) tomatoes, chopped

2 cups (473 mL) dried white beans, soaked overnight in water

Salt, to taste

Freshly ground black pepper, to taste

1. In a soup pot, heat the olive oil and onions. Cook until the onions are soft, about 6 to 7 minutes. Add the garlic and cook for an additional minute, or until the garlic releases its aroma. Add the tomatoes and cook for another 2 minutes, or until the tomatoes give up their liquid. Add the beans and stir to coat them with the oil and the vegetables.

2. Add enough fresh water to cover the beans by about 1½ inches (3.5 cm) and bring to a boil. Reduce the heat to low and cook for at least 1½ hours, or until the beans are done. Add the salt and pepper

White Bean and Escarole Soup

There are many variations of soups featuring beans and greens. They are all easy to make (although not quick, if you are using dried beans) and full of nutrients. They are also full of flavor. Such soups are an integral part of the peasant cuisine of Puglia, as beans and greens grow abundantly in this sunny region. Even in modern times, when meat is more affordable than it has ever been, the Puglian diet remains deeply rooted in vegetables and legumes. Escarole is not a very common green, but it's worth seeking out, as it adds layers of flavor to this simple soup. It is a member of the endive family but is less bitter than many other types of endive and has a complex flavor. Although you can use a different green in this soup (such as dandelion, kale, or even spinach), nothing will give you the same unique flavor that escarole will.

YIELD: 6 SERVINGS

2 cups (473 mL) dried cannellini beans, soaked in water overnight

4 cloves garlic, peeled and cut into large pieces

1 head escarole, washed and roughly chopped

2 tablespoons (30 mL) extra virgin olive oil

1 small yellow onion, peeled and chopped

15 cherry tomatoes, quartered

2 teaspoons (10 mL) red pepper flakes

Salt, to taste

Grated cheese (Caciocavallo or another cheese that melts easily is best, but you can also use pecorino cheese), for serving

Toasted crusty bread, for serving

1. Rinse the soaked beans and put them in a pot with the chopped garlic. Add enough water to cover the beans by 2 inches (5 cm). Bring to a boil, reduce the heat to medium-low, and cook until the beans are tender (about 1½ to 2 hours, depending on how fresh the beans are).

2. When the beans are done, boil the chopped escarole in 1 quart of water until it wilts. Do not drain. Meanwhile, heat the olive oil in a sauté pan. Add the onions and sauté until they are tender. Add the tomatoes and cook another 2 minutes, until the tomatoes release some of their liquid. Add the red pepper flakes. When the onion mixture is cooked, combine it with the cooked escarole and the reserved cooking liquid and add the entire mixture to the cooked beans. Bring to a boil and cook for about 5 minutes for the flavors to blend. Season with salt and add more red pepper, if necessary.

3. Serve hot with the grated cheese and toasted crusty bread.

Chickpea Soup

This soup is simple, delicious, and filling. It is best made with dried beans that have been soaked overnight. The anchovy adds richness without being obvious, and even people who say they do not like anchovies love the layer of flavor they add to this dish. Serve with crusty Puglian bread and good-quality olive oil.

YIELD: 6 SERVINGS

> 2 cups (473 mL) dried chickpeas, soaked in water overnight
>
> 3 cloves garlic, peeled and chopped, divided
>
> 2 tablespoons (30 mL) extra virgin olive oil
>
> 1 anchovy (preferably salt packed), rinsed
>
> 1 tablespoon (15 mL) tomato paste (preferably double concentrated)
>
> 1 teaspoon (5 mL) red pepper flakes
>
> Salt, to taste
>
> Freshly ground black pepper, to taste

1. In a large pot, cover the beans and 2 of the garlic cloves with water. Cook over low heat for 2 to 2½ hours.

2. When the beans are almost done, combine the olive oil, the remaining clove of garlic, and the anchovy in a medium pan. Cook over low heat for a couple of minutes. When the garlic starts to sizzle, add the tomato paste, stir to combine all the ingredients, and remove the pan from the heat.

3. Add the garlic and tomato paste mixture to the beans. Add the red pepper flakes, stir well, and cook for an additional 5 minutes, until the flavors have blended. Add the salt and pepper.

Lentil Soup

Lentils are a great and cheap way to add protein to your diet. They are integral to the cucina povera *(peasant cuisine) of Puglia, where until recently meat was a rarity and the diet consisted mostly of vegetables and legumes. This easy and delicious soup makes a great make-ahead lunch, as it tastes even better the next day. Serve with White Focaccia with Olives (see recipe on page 36) and some cheese.*

YIELD: 4–6 SERVINGS

> 1 (1-pound [450-g]) bag dried lentils
>
> 3 cloves garlic, peeled and halved
>
> ½ onion, quartered and sliced
>
> 2 bay leaves
>
> Salt, to taste
>
> Freshly ground black pepper, to taste
>
> Good-quality olive oil, for drizzling

1. Wash the lentils and put them in a deep pot. Add the garlic, onion, and bay leaves. Add enough water to cover the lentils by about 1 inch (2.5 cm) and bring to a boil. Reduce the heat to low and simmer for 1 hour, or until the lentils are done.

2. Season with the salt and pepper, drizzle some good-quality olive oil on top, and serve hot.

Pasta

Puglian pasta is made with hard (or durum) wheat flour, water, and salt only. This gives it a great texture (chewier than egg-based pasta) and makes it the perfect vehicle for the fresh-tasting, flavorful sauces it is combined with. Orecchiette and cavatelli, which are the most Puglian of pasta shapes, are often sold fresh in stores and markets. In Bari Vecchia (the old part of the port of Bari), the elderly ladies sit outside their front doors making pasta and sell it right there to interested passersby and locals who make special pilgrimages to the Quartiere delle Orecchiette (the Orecciette Quarter).

Orecchiette with Broccoli
See recipe on page 74

Basic Tomato Sauce

This is the most typical southern Italian pasta sauce, infinitely elegant in its simplicity. My friends have embraced this tomato sauce wholeheartedly. It is quick and easy to make, and for those who have kids, it is one of the first recipes they make when their kids are old enough to start cooking. The kids can help break up the canned tomatoes, and they enjoy the delicious sauce without fail. For the parents, this sauce takes the place of store-bought pasta sauces: It is all natural, fresh, and super delicious. It can be used on its own to dress pasta, or it can serve as a base for several other dishes (for example, meatballs with tomatoes and dandelion greens). It is critical that you use fully ripe, high-quality canned tomatoes. I prefer organic canned tomatoes; they are less acidic, because they do not contain the preservative citric acid.

YIELD: 6 SERVINGS

 2 tablespoons (30 mL) extra virgin olive oil

 4 cloves garlic, peeled and thinly sliced

 2 (28-ounce [784-g]) canned whole tomatoes (preferably San Marzano), chopped

 Salt, to taste

 1 teaspoon (5 mL) sugar

1. In a medium pan, heat the olive oil and garlic over low heat. When the garlic starts to sizzle, continue to cook it for a couple of minutes, or until it starts to change color. Do not let the garlic become brown, as that means it is burnt and will taste bitter.

2. Add the tomatoes and their juice and continue cooking at a slow simmer over low heat for 15 to 20 minutes, or until the sauce thickens. As the sauce starts to thicken, season with salt to taste and add the sugar (to balance the acidity of the tomatoes).

Rustic Tomato Sauce

This sophisticated sauce is much richer and more robust than the simple tomato sauce. The anchovy gives it depth of flavor and the olives add a satisfying salty component. The flavors blend perfectly and elevate the basic tomato sauce to new heights. Enjoy it with a bottle of rustic Puglian red, such as Salice Salentino.

YIELD: 6 SERVINGS

6 tablespoons (90 mL) olive oil

3 cloves garlic, peeled and sliced

6 salt- or oil-packed canned anchovies*

¾ cup (177 mL) black olives, chopped

2 (28-ounce [784-g]) cans tomatoes (preferably San Marzano), chopped

Salt, to taste

1. In a large pan, combine the olive oil, garlic, and anchovies. Cook over medium heat until the anchovies are dissolved and the garlic starts to change color. Be careful not to burn the garlic. Add the olives, cook for a minute, and add the tomatoes. Reduce the heat and simmer gently for about 20 minutes, until the flavors have blended. Season with the salt, to taste.

* It is better to use salt-packed anchovies, but they are a little harder to find. If you find them, use fewer, as they are bigger, and make sure to rinse off the salt before sautéing them.

Bucatini with Olives

This simple yet delicious dish exemplifies perfectly the concept of cucina povera *(peasant cuisine). It uses ingredients that are widely available in Puglia and very affordable: olives, olive oil, bread, anchovies, and red pepper. As is the case with many simple Puglian dishes, the whole is a great deal more impressive than the sum of its parts.*

YIELD: 4 SERVINGS

> 7 tablespoons (105 mL) olive oil, divided
>
> ¾ cup (177 mL) fresh breadcrumbs
>
> 4 cloves garlic, peeled and thinly sliced
>
> 6 salt-packed or oil-packed canned anchovies*
>
> 1 teaspoon (5 mL) red pepper flakes
>
> 1 cup (236 mL) green olives, chopped
>
> 11 ounces (308 g) bucatini

1. In a small pan over low heat, warm 1 tablespoon (15 mL) of the olive oil and add the breadcrumbs. Sauté the breadcrumbs until golden. Set aside.

2. In a larger pan over low heat, heat the remaining 6 tablespoons (90 mL) olive oil, the garlic, and the anchovies. As soon as the anchovies have dissolved into the oil and the garlic starts to change color, add the red pepper flakes and olives, toss to coat the olives with the olive oil, and cook for a couple of minutes for the flavors to blend.

3. Meanwhile, cook the pasta in salted water according to the package directions. When the pasta is *al dente*, drain it and add it to the olive mix. Toss to coat the pasta with the sauce. Sprinkle the pasta with the sautéed breadcrumbs and serve hot.

* It is better to use salt-packed anchovies, but they are a little harder to find. If you find them, use fewer, as they are bigger, and make sure to rinse off the salt before sautéing them.

Bucatini with Tomato Sauce and Breadcrumbs

This pasta dish is deeply rooted in Puglian culinary traditions: The breadcrumbs are a substitute for cheese, which for a long time was a luxury for many peasants. The crumbs make the dish richer and more rustic, so this simple dish can satisfy discerning palates while still being very affordable and quick. Serve with a chilled Puglian rosé.

YIELD: 4 SERVINGS

11 ounces (308 g) bucatini

1 recipe Basic Tomato Sauce (see recipe on page 56)

2 tablespoons (30 mL) extra virgin olive oil

¾ cup (177 mL) fresh breadcrumbs (preferably homemade)

Salt, to taste

1. Bring 2 quarts (1.9 L) of water to a boil. Salt the water and add the bucatini. Following the package instructions, cook the pasta to *al dente*.

2. Meanwhile, in a small pan, heat the olive oil over medium-high heat. Add the breadcrumbs and sauté until they start to change color, making sure not to burn them. Set aside.

3. Warm up the tomato sauce and toss it with the bucatini. Add the salt. Sprinkle with the breadcrumbs and serve hot.

Cavatelli

Fresh pasta is one of the most incredible delicacies; making it yourself increases the enjoyment. Puglian pasta does not contain any eggs, and my students are always amazed to discover that a simple combination of flour, salt, and water can yield such great flavor.

Cavatelli (see photo on page 21) is one of the easiest pasta shapes to make—even children enjoy making them. A video is available on olivacooking.com that shows you exactly how to make and shape cavatelli. Watch, practice, and enjoy!

YIELD: 4 SERVINGS

> 1 cup (236 mL) all-purpose flour
> 1 cup (236 mL) semolina flour
> Salt, to taste
> Water, as needed

1. In a bowl, mix together the flours and the salt. Add about ¾ cup (177 mL) of water and start incorporating the water into the flour. As you are mixing, you can add more water, but be careful not to add too much. The dough will gradually absorb the water and become moist.

2. When the dough comes together in a ball, take it out of the bowl and knead it on a flat surface for at least 10 minutes.

3. Wrap the dough in plastic wrap and let it rest for at least 20 minutes. Pinch small pieces of dough (about the size of a marble) and press them with your thumb against a kitchen towel, pushing your thumb away from your body, so each small dough ball is flattened and curls.

4. Cook the fresh pasta in boiled water.

Cavatelli with Beef Roll-Ups

This robust meat sauce is a perfect example of how meat is used in sauces in Puglia—to flavor the sauce, not as the star of the show. The beef in this recipe gets so tender that it crumbles when tossed with the pasta, dressing the pasta perfectly. The trick is to brown the beef rolls really well before adding the wine. This gives the meat a deeper flavor, which permeates the sauce. The sauce pairs great with a robust southern Italian red wine, such as a Salice Salentino Riserva or Aglianico.

YIELD: 4 SERVINGS

½ pound (227 g) sirloin, thinly sliced and pounded ⅛ inch (0.25 cm) thick*

½ cup (118 mL) grated pecorino cheese

4 cloves garlic, peeled and thinly sliced

½ cup (118 mL) finely chopped parsley

Salt, to taste

Freshly ground black pepper, to taste

4 tablespoons (60 mL) extra virgin olive oil

2 cups (473 mL) red wine

1 (28-ounce [784-g]) can tomatoes, chopped

1 recipe Cavatelli (see recipe on page 61) or 11 ounces (308 g) dried cavatelli

1. Place the sirloin slices on a large flat work surface. Evenly divide the pecorino cheese, garlic, and parsley among the sirloin slices, leaving a ½-inch (1-cm) border. Roll up the slices and close them with toothpicks or tie them with kitchen string. Season the roll-ups with salt and pepper.

2. In a large pan, heat the olive oil over medium-high heat. Brown the roll-ups well on all sides, about 3 minutes per side. Add the wine, increase the heat to high, and cook until the wine starts to evaporate. Add the tomatoes, reduce the heat to low, and cook slowly for 2 hours. Toward the end of the cooking time, adjust the seasoning.

3. In a large pot, bring to a boil 4 quarts (3.8 L) of water. Salt the water generously, add the cavatelli, and cook to *al dente*, about 4 minutes. Drain.

4. Toss the pasta with the beef roll-up sauce and serve hot.

* Ask your butcher to slice a sirloin roast thinly.

Cavatelli with Arugula and Olives

Cavatelli with Arugula and Olives (see photo on the next spread) is a very fresh-tasting, summery dish. The flavors are clean, light, and satisfying. It is perfect for a spring or summer lunch—quick and light, yet delicious!

YIELD: 4 SERVINGS

3 tablespoons (45 mL) extra virgin olive oil

3 cloves garlic, peeled and thinly sliced

1 cup (236 mL) black olives, chopped

1 recipe Cavatelli (see recipe on page 61)*

1 (7-ounce [196-g]) bag arugula

¾ cup (177 mL) grated pecorino cheese, for sprinkling

1. In a medium pan, heat the olive oil and garlic over low heat until the garlic starts to turn yellow and releases its aroma. Add the olives and cook for an additional 3 minutes, until the flavors blend.

2. Meanwhile, bring to a boil 4 quarts (3.8 L) of water. Salt the water generously. Add the Cavatelli to the boiling water and cook for about 4 minutes. Add the arugula. Continue cooking for 3 minutes, or until the pasta cooked to *al dente*. Drain and toss in the olive sauce.

3. Sprinkle with pecorino cheese and serve immediately.

* You can substitute dry cavatelli or orecchiette for the fresh cavatelli. If you do so, follow the package instructions for amount and cooking time. Make sure to cook the pasta in well-salted water.

Cavatelli with Arugula and Olives · PAGE 63

Cavatelli with Lamb Sauce

The lamb sauce gives this dish a richness and depth of flavor that makes it perfect for dinner, especially in cooler weather. It pairs well with Salice Salentino, a rustic Puglian red, and some crusty bread.

YIELD: 4 SERVINGS

> 2 tablespoons (30 mL) extra virgin olive oil
>
> Salt, to taste
>
> 1 pound (454 g) lamb stew meat, cut into small cubes
>
> 1 large red onion, peeled, quartered, and thinly sliced
>
> 1 cup (236 mL) dry red wine
>
> 1 (28-ounce [784-g]) can whole tomatoes, chopped
>
> 1 batch Cavatelli (see recipe on page 61) or 11 ounces (308 g) dried cavatelli
>
> Freshly ground black pepper, to taste
>
> ¾ cup (177 mL) grated pecorino cheese, for sprinkling

1. In a heavy saucepan over medium-high heat, heat the olive oil. Salt the lamb, add it to the pan, and brown on all sides, about 7 minutes. Add the onion and cook for another 2 minutes, or until it starts to soften. Add the wine and cook for another 2 minutes, until the alcohol evaporates. Add the tomatoes and their juice. Bring the sauce to a boil, reduce the heat to low, and simmer for at least 1½ hours.

2. Meanwhile, in a large pot, bring to a boil 4 quarts (3.8 L) of water. Salt the water generously, add the cavatelli, and cook to *al dente*, about 4 minutes.

3. Drain the pasta, toss it with the sauce, add the pepper, and serve sprinkled with the pecorino cheese.

Linguine alla Genovese

Despite its name, this dish has nothing to do with the Ligurian city of Genoa. It is, however, popular in much of southern Italy, including Puglia. It is quick and easy and has great flavor. It makes an excellent dinner in the summer or lunch any time of the year. I sometimes serve it with the Chicken Breast Roll-Ups (see recipe on page 114), as the flavors are complementary. Pair this dish with a crisp Puglian white or a rosé.

YIELD: 4 SERVINGS

3 tablespoons (45 mL) extra virgin olive oil

3 large Vidalia onions, peeled, halved, and thinly sliced

1 cup (236 mL) dry white wine

11 ounces (308 g) linguine

Salt, to taste

Freshly ground black pepper, to taste

¾ cup (177 mL) grated pecorino cheese, for sprinkling

1. In a medium pan, heat the olive oil over medium-low heat. Add the onions and cook for 7 to 8 minutes, or until they are soft and have released all of their liquid. Add the wine and cook for another 5 to 6 minutes, or until most of the wine has evaporated.

2. Meanwhile, bring a large pot of salted water to a boil. Add the linguine and cook to *al dente,* according to the package instructions. Drain, reserving some of the cooking water.

3. Toss the linguine with the onion sauce, adding some of the pasta cooking water, if necessary.

4. Add the salt and pepper. Serve hot, sprinkled with the pecorino cheese.

Linguine with Grape Tomatoes and Capers

This simple and easy-to-make dish has all the flavors of Puglia: ripe tomatoes, capers, and olive oil. The flavor is complex, and my guests often find it difficult to believe that the recipe is this simple. Use the best-quality capers you can find—preferably salt packed, as brined capers will change the flavor of the dish slightly. If you are using brined capers, rinse them thoroughly.

YIELD: 4 SERVINGS

4 tablespoons (60 mL) extra virgin olive oil

3 cloves garlic, peeled and thinly sliced

3 tablespoons (45 mL) salt-packed capers, rinsed

1 pint (473 mL) ripe grape or cherry tomatoes, quartered

5 tablespoons (75 mL) fresh breadcrumbs

11 ounces (308 g) dried linguine

1. In a large pan, heat the olive oil and garlic over low heat. When the garlic starts to sizzle, add the capers and toss. Cook for 1 minute. Add the tomatoes and cook for another 5 to 6 minutes, until the tomatoes release some of their liquid. Add the breadcrumbs and cook for an additional 2 to 3 minutes, until they start to change color.

2. Meanwhile, in a large pot of salted water, cook the linguine to *al dente,* according to the package instructions. Drain, reserving a little of the pasta cooking water to thin the sauce, if necessary, and toss with the sauce.

Orecchiette with Three Cheeses

This rich and comforting vegetarian dish is very satisfying and pairs well with a medium-bodied red wine and crusty bread. It makes a perfect Sunday lunch or a worknight dinner, because the tomato sauce can be prepared ahead of time.

YIELD: 4 SERVINGS

⅔ package dried orecchiette (about 2 cups [473 mL])

1 recipe Basic Tomato Sauce (see recipe on page 56)

¾ cup (177 mL) fresh mozzarella cheese, cubed

½ cup (118 mL) provolone cheese, cubed

½ cup (118 mL) grated pecorino cheese, for sprinkling

1. Preheat the oven to 400°F (200°C).

2. In a large pot, bring to a boil 4 quarts (3.8 L) of water. Salt the water generously, add the orecchiette, and cook to *al dente*, according to the package instructions.

3. In a casserole dish, layer the orecchiette with the tomato sauce. Add the mozzarella cheese and provolone cheese and stir to combine.

4. Sprinkle with the pecorino cheese and bake for 15 to 20 minutes, or until the cheese on top forms a crust.

Orecchiette with Arugula Pesto

When made with store-bought pasta, this simple dish takes minutes. It has a very fresh flavor that recalls spring—even in the middle of winter. It is a great way to add something green to your diet and a good way to get children to taste arugula. The pine nuts add richness to the pesto, and the pecorino cheese rounds out that richness. The dish becomes vegan when served without the cheese.

The pesto freezes very well. Take it out of the freezer an hour before you plan to use it and let it thaw at room temperature.

YIELD: 4 SERVINGS

⅔ package dried orecchiette (about 2 cups [473 mL])

1 (7-ounce [196-g]) bag arugula

2 tablespoons (30 mL) pine nuts, toasted

3 tablespoons (45 mL) extra virgin olive oil

Salt, to taste

½ cup (118 mL) grated pecorino cheese, for sprinkling

1. In a large pot, bring to a boil 4 quarts (3.8 L) of water. Salt the water generously, add the orecchiette, and cook to *al dente*, according to the package instructions.

2. In a food processor, combine the arugula, pine nuts, olive oil, and salt to taste, and process until the mixture has a uniform consistency.

3. When the pasta is done, drain it and toss it with the pesto. Sprinkle with the pecorino cheese and serve immediately.

Orecchiette with Broccoli

Orecchiette with Broccoli (see photo on pages 54–55) is likely the most famous Puglian dish, and it's found in many Italian restaurants around the world. Its unique flavor comes from the anchovy, a common ingredient in southern Italian cooking. In Puglia, the dish is not very spicy, but I add more red pepper flakes as I like my food hotter. The dish can be prepared with fresh broccoli as well, but the broccoli will have to be boiled longer. As is typical in Italian cooking, the vegetables are tender rather than crunchy, which makes the broccoli in this dish more of a sauce (similar to pesto) than a vegetable.

YIELD: 4 SERVINGS

4 tablespoons (60 mL) extra virgin olive oil

3 cloves garlic, peeled and thinly sliced

3 canned anchovies

Red pepper flakes, to taste

1 (16-ounce [454-g]) bag frozen broccoli

Salt, to taste

⅔ package dried orecchiette (about 2 cups [473 mL]) or 1 recipe fresh Cavatelli (see recipe page 61)

¾ cup (177 mL) grated pecorino cheese, for sprinkling

1. In a large pan over low heat, heat the olive oil and garlic. As soon as the garlic starts to change color, add the anchovies and break them up with a wooden spoon. Cook for another 2 minutes, until the anchovies melt into the oil. Add the red pepper flakes.

2. Meanwhile, boil the frozen broccoli for 2 minutes. Drain and set aside.

3. *(If using dried orecchiette)* In a large pot, bring to a boil 4 quarts (3.8 L) of water. Salt the water generously and add the orecchiette. About 2 minutes before the pasta is done (when it is still firm on the inside), add the broccoli to the pot and continue cooking. The pasta should be *al dente*. Drain the pasta and broccoli and add it to the garlic and anchovy sauce. Toss over low heat.

(If using fresh cavatelli) In a large pot, bring to a boil 4 quarts (3.8 L) of salted water. When the water starts to boil, add the frozen broccoli. At this point, the water will stop boiling for a couple of minutes as the broccoli starts to thaw. When the water comes back to a boil, add the fresh pasta and cook for another 2 to 3 minutes. The pasta should be *al dente*. Drain the broccoli and pasta and then toss them with the garlic and anchovy sauce.

4. Serve hot, sprinkled with the pecorino cheese.

Orecchiette with Chickpeas

This robust dish is best served in cooler weather. It is full of flavor and has a good balance of protein and carbohydrates. It's a perfect example of cucina povera *(peasant cuisine), food that is simple yet deeply satisfying. The dish pairs well with a robust Salice Salentino.*

YIELD: 4 SERVINGS

2 cups (473 mL) dried chickpeas

1 large carrot, chopped

1 large onion, peeled and chopped

2 cloves garlic, peeled and cut into quarters

11 ounces (308 g) dried orecchiette

2 teaspoons (10 mL) salt

Extra virgin olive oil, for drizzling

1. Soak the chickpeas overnight in water.

2. Drain and rinse the chickpeas. In a large pot, combine the chickpeas, carrot, onion, and garlic. Add water to cover the beans by about 1½ inches (3.5 cm). Add the salt and bring to a boil. Reduce the heat and cook for about 3 hours, until the chickpeas are soft.

3. Add the orecchiette and continue cooking for another 10 minutes, until the pasta is cooked.

4. Serve drizzled with the olive oil.

Orecchiette with Ricotta

This dish could not be any simpler, but it is excellent comfort food. I consider it a variation on macaroni and cheese, with added flair. Serve with a light-bodied red wine for a light dinner. It is critical to get the highest-quality and freshest ricotta you can find. Do not use reduced-fat ricotta, and try to avoid packaged ricotta as well. Most gourmet food stores sell fresh ricotta, which is worlds apart from the ricotta widely available in white plastic tubs. For the adult version of this dish, drizzle it with olio santo, *which makes it truly come to life.*

YIELD: 4 SERVINGS

11 ounces (308 g) dried orecchiette

1½ cups (354 mL) fresh ricotta

Freshly ground black pepper, to taste

Salt, to taste

Olio Santo (see recipe on page 40), for drizzling (optional)

1. In a large pot, bring to a boil 4 quarts (3.8 L) of water. Salt the water generously, add the orecchiette, and cook to *al dente*, according to the package instructions.

2. Drain the pasta and toss it with the ricotta. Season to taste with freshly ground black pepper and the salt. Drizzle about 1 teaspoon (5 mL) of Olio Santo on each serving, if desired.

Orecchiette with Sausages and Red Wine

This variation of the traditional orecchiette with meat sauce is the favorite of Michelle, a great friend and a faithful research assistant for this cookbook. It is best when made with fresh pasta (see recipe for Cavatelli, page 61), but dry pasta works, too. Serve this with broccoli raab, as its bitterness nicely complements the richness of the sausage.

YIELD: 4 SERVINGS

1 tablespoon (15 mL) extra virgin olive oil

2 large turkey sausages, skins removed, crumbled

1 clove garlic, peeled and thinly sliced

1 (28-ounce [784-g]) can tomatoes (preferably San Marzano), chopped

1 cup (236 mL) full-bodied dry red wine (Salice Salentino or Aglianico)

2 teaspoons (10 mL) red pepper flakes

Salt, to taste

Freshly ground black pepper, to taste

1 recipe Cavatelli (see recipe on page 61) or 11 ounces (308 g) dried orecchiette

½ cup (118 mL) grated pecorino cheese, for sprinkling

1. In a large pan, heat the olive oil over medium-high heat. Add the crumbled sausages and brown well, breaking them up with a wooden spoon. Add the garlic and cook for 1 minute, or until the garlic releases its aroma. Add the tomatoes with their juice, the wine, and the red pepper flakes. When the sauce starts to boil, reduce the heat, cover, and simmer for at least 20 minutes. Add salt and pepper to taste.

2. In a large pot, bring to a boil 4 quarts (3.8 L) of water. Salt the water generously, add the pasta, and cook to *al dente*.

3. Toss the cooked pasta with the sauce and sprinkle it with the pecorino cheese.

Penne with Sausage

This simple and quick dish makes a satisfying weeknight dinner. It takes less than 30 minutes to make, and it has the power to turn the most challenging day around and remind you of the benefits and joys of great food.

It pairs well with Salice Salentino and a side of broccoli raab, the bitterness of which perfectly complements the richness of the sausage.

YIELD: 4 SERVINGS

2 tablespoons (30 mL) olive oil

2 large spicy Italian sausages (pork or turkey), crumbled

1 cup (236 mL) dry white wine

2 teaspoons (10 mL) red pepper flakes

11 ounces (308 g) penne

Salt, to taste

¾ cup (177 mL) grated pecorino cheese, for sprinkling

1. In a pan, heat the olive oil over medium-high heat. Add the sausage and cook until browned, breaking it up with a wooden spoon. When the sausage is cooked, add the wine and red pepper flakes and cook until the liquid reduces by about half.

2. Meanwhile, bring to a boil 4 quarts (3.8 L) of water. Salt the water generously and cook the pasta to *al dente*, according to the package instructions.

3. Drain the pasta, reserving a little of the cooking water. Toss the pasta with the sausage. If the dish becomes too dry, add some of the pasta cooking water.

4. Add the salt, to taste. Serve sprinkled with the pecorino cheese.

Spaghetti with Primitivo, Speck, and Smoked Mozzarella

Primitivo is an indigenous Puglian grape that makes a rich and supple red wine that pairs perfectly with many of Puglia's vegetable-based dishes. I first tasted Spaghetti with Primitivo, Speck, and Smoked Mozzarella (see photo on the next spread) at Acqua e Sale in Ostuni on a warm and sunny spring day. I was intrigued by the menu description, and it didn't disappoint. It has an unusual flavor and would make a perfect start to a dinner party.

YIELD: 4 SERVINGS

> 3 tablespoons (45 mL) extra virgin olive oil
>
> 2 ounces (56 g; about 4 slices) speck or thickly sliced prosciutto, cut into squares*
>
> ½ head radicchio, chopped
>
> 1½ cups (354 mL) Primitivo (or other dry) red wine
>
> 11 ounces (308 g) spaghetti
>
> Salt, to taste
>
> 8 ounces (227 g) smoked mozzarella cheese, cubed

1. In a sauté pan, heat the olive oil over medium heat. Add the speck or prosciutto and sauté until it starts to turn crispy. Add the radicchio and cook for an additional 4 minutes, or until it softens. Add the wine and cook for another 5 minutes, or until the wine evaporates a little. Remove the pan from the heat.

2. Bring to a boil 4 quarts (3.8 L) of water. Salt the water generously, add the spaghetti, and cook to *al dente*, following the package directions. Drain the spaghetti, reserving some of the cooking water.

3. Toss the cooked spaghetti with the sauce. Add the salt, to taste. Add the mozzarella cheese and serve hot.

* Use speck if possible, as it tends to dry out less but has the same rich flavor as prosciutto.

Spaghetti with Primitivo, Speck, and Smoked Mozzarella · **PAGE 79**

Spaghetti with Breadcrumbs and Anchovies

This simple dish tastes very rich and is full of flavor. The anchovies deepen its flavor, and the breadcrumbs provide a texture contrast that is as satisfying and crunchy as it is surprising.

YIELD: 4 SERVINGS

4 tablespoons (60 mL) extra virgin olive oil, divided

1 clove garlic, peeled and thinly sliced

3 salt-packed anchovies, rinsed and deboned

½ cup (118 mL) fresh breadcrumbs

Salt, to taste

11 ounces (308 g) spaghetti

1. In a medium skillet, heat 2 tablespoons (30 mL) of the olive oil, the garlic, and the anchovies over low heat. Break up the anchovy fillets with a wooden spoon. When the garlic starts to change color and the anchovies have melted into the oil, remove the pan from the heat.

2. In a small skillet, heat the remaining 2 tablespoons (30 mL) of olive oil over low heat and add the breadcrumbs. Stir and toast the breadcrumbs until they become golden.

3. Bring to a boil 4 quarts (3.8 L) of water. Salt the water generously, add the pasta, and cook to *al dente*, according to the package instructions.

4. Toss the pasta with the garlic and anchovy mixture. Add the salt, to taste. Sprinkle with the breadcrumbs, and serve immediately.

Spaghetti with Pecorino Cheese and Black Pepper

This is a perfect workday dinner—it's quick, it's simple, and it uses ingredients that most of us have readily available in the pantry and fridge. Try to get the freshest pecorino cheese you can. Aged pecorino does not melt as well and will change the flavor of the dish. Other soft cheeses that melt well would also work, but the flavor will be different.

Pair this dish with a medium-bodied and earthy Puglian red, such as Salice Salentino or Copertino.

YIELD: 4 SERVINGS

11 ounces (3.8 g) spaghetti

2 tablespoons (30 mL) extra virgin olive oil

8 ounces (227 g) fresh pecorino cheese, grated

Salt, to taste

Freshly ground black pepper, to taste

1. Bring to a boil 4 quarts (3.8 L) of water. Salt the water generously, add the spaghetti, and cook to *al dente*, according to the package instructions. Drain the spaghetti, reserving some of the cooking water.

2. In a pan, heat the olive oil over medium-low heat and add the spaghetti. Add the pecorino cheese, salt, and pepper and toss to combine. If the pasta is too dry, add a couple of tablespoons (30 mL) of the cooking water. Serve immediately.

Spaghetti with Zucchini and Pecorino Cheese

This is one of my all-time favorite dishes: light, quick to prepare, and full of flavor. Until I discovered this dish and zucchini frittata, I was not a big fan of zucchini. But this dish makes zucchini shine. When zucchini arrive at the farmer's market in great quantities in the summer, this is the perfect way to enjoy them. I first tasted this dish on a warm summer day in a garden in Puglia. Since then, I have tasted variants of it in other parts of the Italian south, but the Puglian recipe is somewhat lighter. The dish is perfect as a spring or summer lunch or as the opening course of a multicourse dinner. It is quick and easy to make and the flavor will impress. It pairs beautifully with a chilled Puglian rosé.

Yield: 4 servings

> 5 tablespoons (75 mL) extra virgin olive oil
>
> 3 medium zucchini, halved lengthwise and thinly sliced
>
> 1 large onion, peeled and chopped
>
> 1 cup (236 mL) dry white wine
>
> Salt, to taste
>
> Freshly ground black pepper, to taste
>
> 11 ounces (308 g) spaghetti
>
> 1 cup (236 mL) grated pecorino cheese, for sprinkling

1. In a large pan, heat the olive oil over medium heat. Add the zucchini and onions and cook for about 5 minutes, or until the vegetables are soft. Add the wine, increase the heat to high, and continue cooking for another 2 minutes, or until most of the wine has evaporated. Season with the salt and pepper.

2. Bring to a boil 4 quarts (3.8 L) of water. Salt the water generously, add the spaghetti, and cook to *al dente*, following the package directions. Drain and toss with the vegetable sauce.

3. Serve hot, sprinkled with the pecorino cheese.

Timbale

This rich and rustic pasta dish is a favorite of both adults and kids. Kids enjoy eating it and love to help prepare it. There are no strict rules for combining the ingredients, so just have fun. It is a great Sunday night meal, and any leftovers reheat perfectly when sprinkled with a little water. Serve with a green salad and some rustic Salice Salentino.

YIELD: 6 SERVINGS

For the Sauce:

2 tablespoons (30 mL) extra virgin olive oil

1 medium onion, peeled and chopped

2 tablespoons (30 mL) tomato paste

2 (28-ounce [784-g]) cans tomatoes, chopped

1½ cups (354 mL) dry red wine

1. In a large pan, heat the olive oil over medium-low. Add the onion and cook for 4 to 5 minutes, or until soft. Add the tomato paste and cook for another 2 minutes. Add the tomatoes and their juice and bring to a boil. Add the wine, return to a boil, reduce the heat to low, and simmer for at least 1 hour (and up to 2 hours).

For the Timbale:

2 tablespoons (30 mL) extra virgin olive oil

15 small Meatballs (see recipe on page 125)

½ pound (227 g) ham, cubed

8 ounces (227 g) mozzarella cheese, cubed

3 hard-boiled eggs, chopped

1 package tubular pasta, cooked *al dente*

½ cup (118 mL) breadcrumbs

½ cup (118 mL) grated pecorino cheese, for sprinkling

1. Preheat the oven to 400°F (200°C).

2. Brush the bottom and sides of a large casserole dish with the olive oil. In a large bowl, combine the sauce, meatballs, ham, mozzarella cheese, eggs, and cooked pasta and stir to combine. Pour this mixture into the casserole dish. Sprinkle with the breadcrumbs and pecorino cheese and bake for 30 minutes or until a golden crust forms.

3. Serve hot.

Squid Ink Pasta with Dandelion Greens and Beans

Squid Ink Pasta with Dandelion Greens and Beans (see photo on the next spread) is the vegetarian version of a recipe my friend Marilea of Osteria Piazzetta Cattedrale in Ostuni created for me. The dish is well balanced, and the flavors complement each other perfectly. It makes a perfect light lunch and pairs well with a Puglian rosé or a light red.

YIELD: 4 SERVINGS

1 bunch dandelion greens

4 tablespoons (60 mL) extra virgin olive oil

2 cloves garlic, thinly sliced

2 cups (473 mL) cooked white beans

16 ounces (454 g) squid ink pasta*

1. Cut the dandelion greens into bite-sized pieces and boil in salted water for 2 to 3 minutes, or until wilted. Drain and set aside.

2. In a large pan, heat the olive oil and garlic over low heat. When the garlic starts to sizzle, add the beans and greens and toss to combine.

3. Meanwhile, cook the squid ink pasta in a large pot of salted water according to the package directions. Drain, reserving a little of the cooking liquid.

4. Toss the pasta with the greens and beans and serve immediately.

* This dish tastes divine with fresh squid ink pasta, the way Marilea prepares it. Because fresh squid ink pasta is difficult to find in the United States, I make it with dried squid ink pasta, which you can find in gourmet grocery stores.

Squid Ink Pasta with Dandelion Greens and Beans · PAGE 87

Spaghetti with Tomato Sauce, Pine Nuts, and Raisins

This simple tomato sauce reflects the influence of north Africa on the cooking of southern Italy. It has two ingredients that are not too common in Puglian cooking: pine nuts and raisins. The pine nuts give it a rich and nutty flavor, and the raisins adds a subtle sweetness that complements the acidity of the tomatoes. And once again, the secret ingredient—anchovies—gives the sauce richness and flavor.

YIELD: 4 SERVINGS

4 tablespoons (60 mL) extra virgin olive oil, divided

4 tablespoons (60 mL) fresh breadcrumbs

2 cloves garlic, peeled and thinly sliced

2 anchovies

1 (28-ounce [784-g]) can tomatoes (preferably San Marzano), chopped

⅓ cup (79 mL) pine nuts, lightly toasted

¼ cup (59 mL) raisins, soaked for 10 minutes in warm water

Red pepper flakes, to taste (optional)

Salt, to taste

11 ounces (308 g) spaghetti

1. In a small frying pan, heat 2 tablespoons (30 mL) of the olive oil over medium-low heat. Add the breadcrumbs and toast until they turn golden brown. Set aside.

2. In a large pan, heat the remaining 2 tablespoons (30 mL) olive oil, the garlic, and the anchovies over low heat. When the anchovies have melted and the garlic starts to sizzle, add the tomatoes. Stir well and cook over medium-low heat for at least 20 minutes to allow the flavors to blend. Add the pine nuts, raisins, and red pepper flakes (if using) and cook for another 2 minutes. Add salt to taste.

3. Bring to a boil 4 quarts (3.8 L) of water. Salt the water generously, add the spaghetti, and cook to *al dente*, following the package directions. Toss the spaghetti with the sauce, add the salt, to taste, and serve hot.

Potatoes

As in many regions that are historically poor, potatoes are quite common in Puglian cuisine. They are often added to meat dishes and pasta, but they can also be combined with vegetables into a variety of light and flavorful dishes. The dishes in this section can be served as side dishes or as meals in their own right.

Tiella
See recipe on pages 94–95

Tiella

This typically Puglian dish has as many variations as there are cooks. The biggest point of contention is whether you use rice, but other ingredients can be added or taken out. This recipe

is based on the tiella Bari, *which contains rice and mussels. I first tasted this dish in a seaside restaurant in Polignano al Mare, a small town south of Bari on the Adriatic coast. I tried to get the restaurant owner to give me the details. She simply shrugged and said, "It's potatoes and mussels," as if anyone would know immediately what went into the dish. Once I got home, I tried to recreate the dish and realized she was right: It was easy, which is something my cooking-class students and friends still find difficult to believe, given how delicious the results are. The dish is the perfect comfort food for summer, as it is light, yet full of flavor. It pairs well with a crisp Puglian rosé.*

YIELD: 4 SERVINGS

1 pound (454 g) mussels

1 cup (236 mL) dry white wine

1 large yellow onion, peeled and thinly sliced

4 large Yukon Gold potatoes, thinly sliced

2 tablespoons (30 mL) extra virgin olive oil

Salt, to taste

10 (about ½ cup [118 mL]) grape tomatoes, quartered

1 cup (236 mL) uncooked white rice

½ cup (118 mL) grated pecorino cheese, for sprinkling

½ cup (118 mL) toasted breadcrumbs, for sprinkling

1. Preheat the oven to 400°F (200°C).

2. Wash the mussels and discard any that are open and will not close when touched. Put the mussels in a medium pan. Add the wine. Cover and cook over medium heat until the mussels are completely open, about 4 to 5 minutes. Remove the pan from the heat and set aside to cool slightly. Using a fork, take the mussels out of the shells and set them aside. Reserve some of the cooking liquid (a combination of wine and sea water from the mussels).

3. In a medium baking dish, arrange a layer of onions, and then a layer of potato slices. Sprinkle with some olive oil and a little salt, and then layer half the tomatoes. Distribute half the rice as evenly as you can on top and add the mussels. Cover the mussels with more rice, tomatoes, and onions and end with a layer of potatoes. Sprinkle the top layer of potatoes with the remaining olive oil, the pecorino cheese, and the breadcrumbs. Pour some of the cooking liquid from the mussels and add water to come almost ¾ of the way up the sides of the dish. Cook for at least an hour, or until the potatoes are done (they should be tender when pierced with a fork).

Potatoes with Pecorino Cheese

This simple potato dish layered with pecorino is in many ways emblematic of Puglia. Not only is pecorino widely used in Puglia, but it often enhances the simplest of dishes, adding a surprising and rich element to simple pastas and vegetables. The liquid in this dish (either milk or chicken broth) keeps the potatoes and cheese moist and gives the finished product a silky texture.

YIELD: 4 SERVINGS

> 2 tablespoons (30 mL) extra virgin olive oil
>
> 4 large Yukon Gold potatoes, peeled and cut into thin slices
>
> 1 cup (236 mL) grated pecorino cheese
>
> Salt, to taste
>
> 1½ cups (354 mL) whole milk*
>
> ½ cup (118 mL) fresh breadcrumbs

1. Preheat the oven to 400°F (200°C).

2. Brush the bottom and sides of an oven-safe dish with the olive oil. Place one layer of potatoes on the bottom and sprinkle with a little pecorino cheese and a dash of salt. Continue layering potatoes and pecorino cheese, finishing with a layer of pecorino cheese. Pour the milk around the sides of the dish.

3. Sprinkle with the breadcrumbs and bake for at least 1 hour, or until a golden brown crust forms on top.

* For a lighter version, use chicken broth instead of milk.

Roasted Potatoes with Breadcrumbs

These potatoes have the power to impress even the most sophisticated gourmets.
The breadcrumbs give the dish a twist no one expects. They pair well with the Beef Roll-Ups
(see recipe on page 131).

(see recipe on page 131).

YIELD: 4 SERVINGS

> 5–6 medium Yukon Gold potatoes, peeled and cubed
>
> 3 tablespoons (45 mL) extra virgin olive oil
>
> 6 tablespoons (90 mL) breadcrumbs
>
> Salt, to taste

1. Preheat the oven to 400°F (200°C).

2. Boil the potatoes in a large pot of salted water until they are about halfway done (if you insert a fork in a piece of potato, the center should offer some resistance). Drain the potatoes and arrange them in a single layer in a large baking dish.

3. Drizzle the potatoes with the olive oil, toss them to coat, and sprinkle them with the breadcrumbs. Bake for at least 20 minutes, or until the potatoes are soft on the inside and crunchy on the outside. Add the salt, to taste, and serve hot.

Potatoes and Peppers

The flavor intensity of this simple yet creative combination is often surprising to my dinner guests and students. The fields of Puglia yield a number of very flavorful peppers that are often added as a side dish, brightening both the color and the flavor of the meal. I use poblano peppers, even though they are not from Puglia, because they have the flavor intensity of Puglian peppers and add spiciness and character to the dish.

YIELD: 4 SERVINGS

> 6 medium potatoes
>
> 2 red bell peppers
>
> 2 poblano peppers*
>
> 5 tablespoons (75 mL) extra virgin olive oil
>
> Salt, to taste
>
> Freshly ground black pepper, to taste

1. Peel the potatoes and cut them into ½-inch (1-cm) cubes. Boil the cubes in salted water for 10 minutes, or until they are soft but not falling apart. Drain and set aside.

2. Cut the peppers into ¼-inch (0.5-cm) strips and cut the strips into bite-sized pieces. In a large pan, heat the olive oil over medium-high heat and add the peppers. Cook for 5 minutes, or until they start to soften. Add the potatoes and cook the pepper–potato mixture for another 3 to 5 minutes, or until the potatoes start to brown.

3. Season with the salt and pepper to taste and serve hot.

* You can use green bell peppers, if you prefer.

Puglian Potatoes

I love potatoes—mashed, scalloped, or simply oven baked. How such a simple and lowly vegetable can turn into creamy lushness continually amazes me. This dish takes potatoes to a new level and adds layers of flavor that make this Cinderella vegetable shine. There are many variations of this dish in Puglia—some with rice, others without. This is one of the simplest versions, and it is perfect by itself or as an accompaniment to roasted fish or meat.

YIELD: 6 SERVINGS

¼ cup (59 mL) olive oil, divided

2 medium yellow onions, peeled and thinly sliced

6 medium Yukon Gold potatoes, peeled and thinly sliced

2 medium tomatoes, sliced

¾ cup (177 mL) breadcrumbs

¾ cup (177 mL) grated pecorino cheese

Salt, to taste

Red pepper flakes, to taste

Olio santo, for drizzling

1. Preheat the oven to 375°F (190°C).

2. In an enameled cast-iron pot, pour half the olive oil and spread it around to cover the bottom of the pot. Layer ⅓ of the sliced onions in the bottom of the pot, add a layer of potatoes and a layer of tomatoes, and sprinkle with some breadcrumbs, cheese, salt, and red pepper flakes. Continue layering, finishing with a layer of breadcrumbs, cheese, and red pepper flakes. Drizzle with the remaining olive oil, pour in enough water to come halfway up the layered vegetables, and bake for about 1½ hours, or until the potatoes are soft.

3. Serve drizzled with some Olio Santo (see recipe on page 40) for heat and spiciness.

Vegetable Potato Stew

This is the perfect one-pot vegetarian dinner. It can also be served with simple roasted chicken or fish. It is light, yet full of flavor. Once again, here is a perfect example of the cucina povera *(peasant cuisine) of Puglia, where widely available vegetables are used in creative ways to produce dishes of uncommon richness and flavor.*

YIELD: 4 SERVINGS

6 small to medium potatoes (1½ to 2 pounds [681–908 g]), peeled and cubed

6 canned tomatoes, chopped

1 medium onion, peeled and chopped

3 cloves garlic, peeled and thinly sliced

2 tablespoons (30 mL) extra virgin olive oil

1½ cups (354 mL) water

½ cup (118 mL) black olives, chopped

Salt, to taste

½ cup (118 mL) grated pecorino cheese, for sprinkling

1. In a large pan, combine the potatoes, tomatoes, onion, garlic, olive oil, and water. Cook, covered, over medium-high heat, until the potatoes are done. If the dish starts to dry out and stick to the bottom of the pan, add more water.

2. Uncover the pan, add the olives, and cook for an additional minute. Season with salt to taste, keeping in mind that the pecorino cheese will add more saltiness.

3. Sprinkle with pecorino cheese and enjoy!

Fish and Seafood

Puglia has 800 miles of coastline that yields seafood of all kinds: from sea urchins—served raw, grilled, or over pasta—to squid, octopus, mussels, and fish both big and small that melt in the mouth when prepared simply and enjoyed with some chilled Puglian rosé.

Baked Fish with Potatoes
See recipe on page 105

Baked Fish

The beauty of this dish is that it can taste many different ways, depending on the fish you use. It is light and flavorful, and because of its simplicity, the fish shines in all its glory. So, choose your favorite fish and you will have a great dinner in no time.

YIELD: 4 SERVINGS

2 large lemons, thinly sliced

4 medium whole fish (preferably white fleshed), cleaned

1 cup (236 mL) black olives, halved

4 cloves garlic, peeled and quartered

½ cup (118 mL) flat-leaf parsley, chopped

4 tablespoons (60 mL) extra virgin olive oil

1. Preheat the oven to 375°F (191°C).

2. Cover the bottom of a large baking dish with lemon slices. Place the fish on top of the lemon slices. Distribute the olives, garlic, and parsley equally among the four fish, placing them inside the cavities. Pour about 1 tablespoon (15 mL) olive oil on each fish and rub it all over.

3. Bake for 15 to 20 minutes.

Baked Fish with Potatoes

This one-pot dish (see photo on pages 102–103) makes a perfect summer meal. It pairs beautifully with a Puglian rosé or any lighter white wine.

YIELD: 4 SERVINGS

4 fillets flaky white fish (cod, halibut, or other white fish)*

½ cup (118 mL) extra virgin olive oil, divided

1 yellow onion, peeled and chopped

1 clove garlic, peeled and thinly sliced

1 teaspoon (5 mL) red pepper flakes

1 tablespoon (15 mL) salt-packed capers, rinsed

1 cup (236 mL) dry white wine

4 medium potatoes, peeled and cut into small cubes

1. Preheat the oven to 400°F (200°C).

2. Wash the fish fillets and pat them dry with a paper towel. Set aside.

3. In a large pan, heat 3 tablespoons (45 mL) of the olive oil over medium-high heat. Add the onion and cook until soft (but not brown). Add the garlic and red pepper flakes. Toss together and cook for another minute. Add the capers and wine and cook until the wine is reduced by a third.

4. Brush the bottom of a large baking dish with the remaining olive oil. Distribute the fish and potatoes evenly. Pour the onion and wine mixture over the fish and potatoes, cover, and cook for about 15 minutes, or until the fish is cooked through and the potatoes are soft.

* If the fish fillets are thin and cook faster than the potatoes, transfer them to a heated plate and cover them with foil while you finish cooking the potatoes on the stovetop. If the liquid evaporates completely, add a little warm water.

Octopus Stew

I first tasted this delicious stew in a seaside restaurant in Gallipoli and was instantly won over. The octopus was tender and flavorful, and the potatoes were soft and creamy. It is a dish that always reminds me of summer: The salinity of the octopus brings back the sea on that sunny day, and the flavor of the wine reminds me of the ripe Puglian grapes basking in the sun.

Baby octopus is available in grocery stores year round, cleaned and ready to cook. Because the wine becomes concentrated in the cooking process, use the best wine you can. Pair the dish with the wine you use for cooking or a nice Puglian rosé.

YIELD: 4 SERVINGS

2 tablespoons (30 mL) olive oil

1 medium onion, peeled and roughly chopped

1¼ pounds (568 g) baby octopus, cut into bite-sized pieces

4 large Yukon Gold potatoes, cut into ½-inch (1-cm) cubes

2 cups (473 mL) white wine

Salt, to taste

1. In a medium soup pot, heat the olive oil over medium heat. Add the onion and cook until soft. Add the octopus, potatoes and wine and bring to a boil over high heat. Reduce the heat and simmer slowly for 1 hour.

2. Serve hot.

Salt Cod (in Tomato Sauce) with Potatoes

Salt cod is usually considered a northern Italian ingredient, but it is occasionally used in Puglian dishes, especially in the winter. It is heartier than fresh fish and has a much stronger flavor. You can find salt cod in large supermarkets; if your market does not carry it regularly, it can order it for you. Salt cod can keep for a while in the fridge before it is soaked, so I usually have some on hand in the winter. Salt-cod stews such as this one are full of flavor yet also light. They make perfect comfort food in the colder months.

YIELD: 4 SERVINGS

1 pound (454 g) salt cod

2 tablespoons (30 mL) extra virgin olive oil

1 medium yellow onion, peeled and chopped

1 (28-ounce [784-g]) can tomatoes (preferably San Marzano), chopped

1 cup black olives, coarsely chopped

4 medium Yukon Gold potatoes, peeled, cubed, and boiled until almost done

Salt, to taste

Freshly ground black pepper, to taste

2 tablespoons (30 mL) chopped Italian parsley (optional), for sprinkling

1. Soak the cod in cold water (in the refrigerator) for at least 24 hours, changing the water twice.

2. Preheat the oven to 400°F (200°C).

3. In a large, oven-safe pan, heat the olive oil over medium-high heat. Add the onion and cook for about 4 minutes, until soft. Add the tomatoes and their juice and cook for another 5 minutes, until the tomato sauce starts to thicken. Add the olives and the fish, decrease the heat to medium-low, and cook for 15 minutes. Add the potatoes and finish cooking in the oven for 10 minutes.

4. Taste and add salt and pepper, if necessary. Sprinkle with the parsley and serve hot.

Stuffed Squid

Puglia has more than 500 miles (800 km) of coastline, and you can find all kinds of delicacies from the sea in the towns and villages that line the coast. A few miles inland, however, seafood disappears and is replaced by more land-based dishes. One sea delicacy that you do find even inland is cuttlefish or squid, most often stuffed and baked.

This recipe is simple and easy to prepare, a fact my friends who helped me test it found difficult to believe. Squid is not hard to find in U.S. grocery stores, and it is relatively affordable, compared with other seafood.

Pair this dish with a Puglian rosé and wow your friends.

YIELD: 4 SERVINGS

½ cup (118 mL) fresh breadcrumbs

⅓ cup (79 mL) grated pecorino cheese

1 tablespoon (15 mL) capers, chopped

1 clove garlic, peeled and chopped

1 egg, lightly beaten

8 small to medium squid, cleaned

2 tablespoons (30 mL) extra virgin olive oil

½ teaspoon (2.5 mL) salt

1. Preheat the oven to 350°F (180°C).

2. In a small bowl, combine the breadcrumbs, pecorino cheese, capers, garlic, and egg and stir to combine. Divide the stuffing among the 8 squid, filling them with a small spoon. Do not pack the stuffing too firmly into the squid.

3. Arrange the squid close together in a baking dish or on a baking sheet. Drizzle with the olive oil and sprinkle with the salt.

4. Bake for 1 hour.

Poultry

I love seeing the expressions on my friends' faces when they taste the dishes in this section. They all agree that chicken and turkey have never tasted this great! Puglian chicken and turkey dishes may be the pinnacle of creativity: a dash of pecorino cheese adds layers of flavor to a simple chicken and potato dish and capers give turkey a whole new identity. From quick and simple dishes—like the chicken with prosciutto—that can be prepared on any night to rich and robust dishes—like the chicken with tomatoes and red wine and the peasant chicken—the recipes in this section make poultry intriguing again.

Chicken with Potatoes
See recipe on page 112

111

Chicken with Potatoes

My friend Paola, a native of Ostuni, shared her grandmother's recipe for meat and potatoes with me. This recipe can also be made with lamb—see the variation on page 130. If you are preparing the dish with chicken (see photo on pages 110–111), it is very important to use free-range chicken, which has more flavor. As Paola says, the secret is in how well you rub the ingredients into the chicken and potatoes, and the best tools to use are your hands. The dish is simple to make and perfect for entertaining, as you can assemble it ahead of time and pop it in the oven when your guests arrive. You'll be able to enjoy your guests' company while preparing a meal everyone is sure to love.

YIELD: 4 SERVINGS

> 3 free-range chicken legs, skin on
>
> 3 free-range chicken thighs, skin on, halved
>
> Juice of ½ lemon
>
> 4 medium Yukon Gold potatoes, peeled and cut into strips
>
> ½ cup (118 mL) extra virgin olive oil
>
> ½ cup (118 mL) dry white wine
>
> ½ cup (118 mL) grated pecorino cheese
>
> Salt, to taste

1. Preheat the oven to 400°F (200°C).

2. Place the chicken pieces in a large bowl of water. Add the lemon juice. Let sit for 30 minutes. Wash the chicken well, drain it, and pat it dry.

3. In a baking dish, combine the chicken, potatoes, oil, and wine. Sprinkle with the pecorino cheese and salt. Using your hands, mix together all the ingredients, making sure to rub the oil, salt, and pecorino cheese into the chicken and potatoes.

4. Bake, uncovered, for 1 hour and 15 minutes. Serve hot.

Peasant Chicken

This simple and delicious peasant dish is perfect with Potatoes and Peppers (see recipe on page 98). Its simple flavors pair well with a rosé or a light red wine.

page 98

YIELD: 4 SERVINGS

> 4 pieces chicken, bone in, skinless
>
> Salt, to taste
>
> 4 tablespoons (60 mL) extra virgin olive oil
>
> 2 medium onions, peeled and sliced
>
> 2 garlic cloves, peeled and thinly sliced
>
> Fresh rosemary, to taste
>
> Fresh sage, to taste
>
> 2 cups (473 mL) dry white wine

1. Wash the chicken, pat it dry, and season it with salt on all sides.

2. In a heavy skillet, heat the olive oil over medium-high heat. Add the chicken and brown well on all sides, about 12 minutes total. Add the onions and continue to cook for another minute. Add the garlic, rosemary, and sage and cook for another minute, or until the garlic releases its aroma.

3. Add the wine and scrape any brown bits from the bottom of the pan. Reduce the heat to a slow simmer, cover, and simmer for 20 minutes.

4. Serve hot.

Chicken Breast Roll-Ups with Prosciutto and Pecorino Cheese

The prosciutto gives this simple dish richness and makes it perfect even for fancy dinners. Speck is similar to prosciutto but usually a little more moist. Use speck if possible, as it tends to dry out less and has the same rich flavor as prosciutto. This dish pairs well with a fuller-bodied Puglian rosé (from Negroamaro) or a light- to medium-bodied red.

YIELD: 4 SERVINGS

4 chicken breast filets, pounded to ¼ inch (0.5 cm) thickness

4 slices prosciutto or speck

1 cup (236 mL) grated pecorino cheese

3 tablespoons (45 mL) extra virgin olive oil

1 cup (236 mL) dry white wine

Salt, to taste

1. On a clean working surface, spread out the pounded chicken filets. Cover each with a slice of prosciutto and sprinkle with ¼ of the pecorino cheese. Roll up each filet and close it with a toothpick. Set aside.

2. In a large pan, heat the olive oil over medium-high heat. Add the roll-ups and cook for about 3 minutes on each side, until they are well browned on all sides. Add the wine, scrape the bottom of the pan to loosen any pieces of meat, reduce the heat, and cook for 10 minutes. Add salt, to taste.

Chicken with Prosciutto

The combination of ingredients in this dish exalts the chicken breast and makes it more interesting while keeping it healthy. The prosciutto adds richness of flavor, and the onions and wine add moisture and freshness. The end result is a chicken breast that even dedicated red-meat lovers will embrace enthusiastically.

YIELD: 4 SERVINGS

> 2 tablespoons (30 mL) extra virgin olive oil
>
> 4 slices prosciutto, chopped
>
> 1 small onion, peeled, quartered, and thinly sliced
>
> 4 chicken breasts, bone in and skin on
>
> Salt, to taste
>
> 2 cups (473 mL) dry white wine

1. In a large pan, heat the olive oil over medium heat. Add the prosciutto and cook for 2 minutes, or until it starts to crisp up. Add the onions and cook for an additional 2 minutes, until they begin to soften.

2. Season the chicken breasts with salt. Push the prosciutto and onions to the side of the pan and add the chicken breasts, skin side down. Brown well on all sides, about 12 minutes total.

3. Add the wine and cook until it starts to evaporate. Reduce the heat and simmer slowly for about 20 minutes, until the chicken is cooked through (depending on how thick the chicken breasts are, you might have to cook them a little longer).

4. Serve hot, drizzled with the prosciutto and onion sauce.

Chicken with Tomatoes and Red Wine

This delectable chicken stew can double as sauce for fresh pasta. It is rich and full of flavor without being heavy. The chicken falls off the bone and can be shredded to make pasta sauce. The flour and red wine give the dish a richness that makes it perfect for cold winter nights.

The stew pairs well with a more robust Puglian red, such as Salice Salentino or Copertino.

YIELD: 4 SERVINGS

3 tablespoons (45 mL) extra virgin olive oil

1 medium onion, peeled and chopped

2 cloves garlic, peeled and finely chopped

6 pieces chicken, bone in and skin on

2 teaspoons (10 mL) all-purpose flour

2 cups (473 mL) dry red wine

8 canned tomatoes, chopped

Salt, to taste

Freshly ground black pepper, to taste

1. In a large pan, heat the olive oil over medium heat. Add the onion and cook until it starts to soften, about 5 minutes. Add the garlic and cook for another minute.

2. Add the chicken, skin side down, and cook until it is browned on all sides, 8 to 12 minutes total. Sprinkle the chicken with the flour, stir, and add the wine. Increase the heat to high and cook until the wine reduces by about half. Add the tomatoes, 1 cup (236 mL) of water, salt, and pepper and bring to a boil.

3. Reduce the heat to low and cook, covered, for 40 minutes.

Turkey Breast Roll

Turkey breast is a perfect alternative to chicken. The flavor is different enough to make poultry interesting again! Turkey breast roll is a good alternative to Thanksgiving turkey if you are cooking for a small party. It also makes a perfect Sunday dinner and is even delicious served cold in sandwiches.

YIELD: 8 SERVINGS

2 pounds (908 g) turkey breast, skin on, boneless

4 slices prosciutto

½ 16-ounce bag frozen spinach, boiled and squeezed dry

½ cup (118 mL) grated pecorino cheese

Salt, to taste

2 tablespoons (30 mL) extra virgin olive oil

1½ cups (354 mL) dry white wine

1. Preheat the oven to 350°F (180°C).

2. On a flat surface, place the turkey breast skin side down and pound it until it is of equal thickness throughout (about ½ inch [1 cm]).

3. Cover the turkey breast with slices of prosciutto. Distribute the cooked spinach evenly on top of the prosciutto, leaving a ½-inch (1-cm) border on all sides, and sprinkle with the pecorino cheese. Roll the breast tightly and tie it with kitchen string. Season with salt on the outside.

4. In a large, oven-safe pan, heat the olive oil over medium-high heat. Add the turkey roll-up and brown on all sides, about 12 minutes. Add the wine and cook for 2 minutes, until it starts to evaporate. Cover the pan with foil, transfer it to the oven, and bake for 25 minutes, or until the internal temperature of the meat reaches 165°F (74°C). Use a meat thermometer to make sure the turkey does not overcook.

Turkey Breast with Capers and White Wine

This simple and quick dish packs a lot of flavor. It is a wonderful way to make turkey the star of the show. Since it has a strong flavor, it is best served with simple roasted potatoes or potatoes with breadcrumbs. The capers make the dish more interesting and never fail to make me long for the warm and sunny Italian south.

YIELD: 4 SERVINGS

½ cup (118 mL) all-purpose flour

1½ teaspoons (7.5 mL) salt

½ teaspoon (2.5 mL) freshly ground black pepper

1 pound (454 g) turkey breast, cut into slices ½-inch (1-cm) thick and 1-inch (2.5-cm) wide

2 tablespoons (30 mL) extra virgin olive oil

1 cup (236 mL) dry white wine

2 tablespoons (30 mL) salt-packed capers, rinsed

2 tablespoons (30 mL) lemon juice

1. On a plate, combine the flour, salt, and pepper. Roll the turkey pieces around in the seasoned flour. Shake off any excess flour.

2. In a large pan, heat the olive oil over medium-high heat. Add the turkey pieces and cook until they are golden brown on both sides, about 3 to 4 minutes per side. Add the wine and cook until it is reduced by half. Add the capers and lemon juice and cook for another 2 to 3 minutes.

3. Serve hot, drizzled with the wine and lemon juice sauce.

Meat

M eat was historically scarce in Puglia: Cooks used it as a condiment, rather than as the star of the show. Because Puglia has a rich shepherding tradition, to this day lamb is one of the more common meats. It is the centerpiece of every Easter meal and adds richness to many celebrations. In modern times, beef has also become more available and more affordable, but it is still used more often in sauces (to enrich them) than on its own.

Lamb with Fresh Peas
See recipe on page 124

Lamb with Fresh Peas

Young lamb, usually served with fresh peas, is the traditional Easter dish in Puglia. Good butcher shops or lamb farms in the United States feature young lamb in March and April. If you cannot find young lamb, make Lamb with Fresh Peas (see photo on pages 122-123) with regular lamb, but cook it twice as long. This dish pairs perfectly with mashed potatoes (preferably made with olive oil) and a medium- to full-bodied red, such as an Aglianico or a robust Negroamaro.

YIELD: 4 SERVINGS

> 3 tablespoons (45 mL) extra virgin olive oil
>
> 1 large onion, peeled, quartered, and thinly sliced
>
> 1½ pounds (681 g) young lamb (shoulder cut), cubed
>
> ½ teaspoon (2.5 mL) salt, plus more, to taste
>
> 1 cup (236 mL) dry white wine
>
> 1 pound (454 g) frozen peas
>
> Freshly ground black pepper, to taste
>
> ½ cup (118 mL) grated pecorino cheese

1. In a large Dutch oven, heat the olive oil over medium heat. Add the onion and cook until softened, about 5 to 6 minutes.

2. Wash the lamb. Pat it dry with a paper towel and season it with the salt.

3. Add the lamb to the Dutch oven and cook until it is browned on all sides, about 10 to 12 minutes.

3. Add the wine to the Dutch oven and cook until the alcohol evaporates and the wine reduces by almost half, about 4 minutes.

4. Reduce the heat to low, cover, and cook for about 1 hour. (The lamb should fall apart when pierced with a fork. If you are using regular lamb, cook it for at least 2 hours over very low heat.)

5. When the lamb is almost done, add the peas and cook for about 5 minutes, until the flavors blend.

6. Season with the salt and pepper to taste. Sprinkle with the pecorino cheese and serve hot.

Meatballs with Tomato Sauce and Greens

This Puglian version of the ubiquitous meatballs in tomato sauce is made interesting by the addition of dandelion greens. The greens add an element of texture and a slight bitterness, which counteracts the sweetness of the meatballs. Serve Meatballs with Tomato Sauce and Greens (see photo on the next spread) with a medium-bodied red wine, such as Negroamaro or Nero di Troia.

YIELD: 6 SERVINGS

½ pound (277 g) ground beef

½ pound (277 g) ground pork

1 egg

1 large slice country bread, soaked in milk, squeezed dry, and torn into pieces

½ cup (118 mL) grated pecorino cheese

½ cup (118 mL) finely chopped parsley

Salt, to taste

Freshly ground black pepper, to taste

½ cup (118 mL) extra virgin olive oil

1 bunch dandelion greens, washed and cut into bite-sized pieces

1 recipe Basic Tomato Sauce (see recipe on page 56)

Pasta or fresh bread for serving

1. In a large bowl, combine the ground beef, ground pork, egg, bread pieces, pecorino cheese, parsley, salt, and pepper. Mix until just combined (do not overmix). Tear off golf-ball–sized pieces and shape them into meatballs.

2. In a large pan, heat the olive oil over medium-high heat. When the oil is hot (but not smoking), add the meatballs to the pan and cook them until they are browned on all sides.* Remove them from the pan and place them on a paper towel to drain.

3. Bring a large stockpot of salted water to a boil. Add the dandelion greens and boil for 2 minutes, or until the greens start to wilt. Remove the stockpot from the heat and transfer the greens to a strainer. Discard the water.

4. In the now-empty stockpot, combine the tomato sauce and the cooked greens and bring to a boil. Add the hot meatballs. Stir the mixture together and cook for 2 minutes. Serve hot, either over pasta or in the form of meatball sandwiches on fresh bread.

* If you prefer, you can instead bake the meatballs in the oven at 375°F (190°C) for 20 to 30 minutes (depending on size), until they are brown on top.

Meatballs with Tomato Sauce and Greens · PAGE 125

Lamb Stew (Stracotto)

This simple lamb stew, which requires minimal preparation time, is made richer and more delicious by the addition of pecorino cheese, a surprising ingredient in Puglian cuisine. This one-pot dish, which grew out of a Puglian shepherd tradition, will impress even those who aren't already fans of lamb. The tomatoes add freshness and acidity, and the pecorino cheese perfumes the dish and tantalizes the taste buds. Pair with a full-bodied and robust red, such as Aglianico.

Note: Good butcher shops or lamb farms in the United States feature young lamb in March and April. If you cannot find young lamb, make the dish with regular lamb, but cook it twice as long.

YIELD: 4 SERVINGS

2 tablespoons (30 mL) extra virgin olive oil

1 pound (454 g) young lamb, cut into ½-inch (1-cm) pieces

Salt, to taste

1 large yellow onion, peeled and sliced

15 cherry tomatoes, halved

½ cup (118 mL) pecorino cheese, cubed

Freshly ground black pepper, to taste

Mashed or roasted potatoes, for serving

1. In a large Dutch oven, heat the olive oil over medium-high heat. Season the lamb with salt, place it in the Dutch oven, and brown on all sides, about 10 minutes total.

2. Add the onion, tomatoes, and cheese to the Dutch oven and mix, scraping the bottom of the pan to release any meat bits that are stuck. Add 3 cups (708 mL) of water, reduce the heat, and simmer slowly for 1½ hours.

3. Season with the salt and pepper to taste. Serve hot over mashed potatoes or with simple roasted potatoes.

Lamb with Potatoes

This variation of my friend Paola's Chicken with Potatoes (see recipe on page 112) has a rich and very different flavor. It pairs well with a full-bodied red wine, such as Aglianico.

YIELD: 4 SERVINGS

4 medium Yukon Gold potatoes, peeled and cut into strips

1½ pounds (681 g) lamb shoulder, cut into pieces

½ cup (118 mL) extra virgin olive oil

½ cup (118 mL) dry white wine

½ cup (118 mL) grated pecorino cheese, for sprinkling

Salt, to taste

Freshly ground black pepper, to taste

1. Preheat the oven to 400°F (200°C).

2. In a large baking dish, combine the potatoes, lamb, oil, and wine. Sprinkle with the pecorino cheese, salt, and pepper.

3. Mix everything together with your hands, making sure to rub the oil, pecorino cheese, salt, and pepper well into the lamb and potatoes.

4. Bake, uncovered for 1 hour and 15 minutes. Serve hot.

Beef Roll-Ups

Fabio, a friend of a friend who lives in Ostuni and loves to cook his family recipes, shared this one with me. One sunny spring day, Fabio and I made some of his mother's recipes and then shared the results with a group of friends. It remains one of my fondest memories: When I think of that day, I can taste the tender meat and the soft, creamy scamorza cheese oozing out of it. This recipe uses smoked mozzarella cheese, as scamorza is difficult to find in the United States. Serve with the Roasted Potatoes and Breadcrumbs (see recipe on page 97) and a full-bodied red wine, such as a good Aglianico or the Salice Salentino Riserva.

YIELD: 6 SERVINGS

6 thin slices sirloin*

6 slices speck or prosciutto

2 ounces (56 g) smoked mozzarella cheese, cut into long sticks, about ¼-inch (.5-cm) thick

3 tablespoons (45 mL) extra virgin olive oil

1 medium onion, peeled and chopped

1½ cups (354 mL) dry white wine

1 cup (236 mL) tomato juice (the juice from 1 [14-ounce (392-g)] can tomatoes)

Salt, to taste

Freshly ground black pepper, to taste

1. Place the slices of beef on a clean work surface. Cover them with plastic wrap and pound them to a ⅛-inch (0.25-cm) thickness.

2. Place a slice of speck on each slice of beef. Put a piece of mozzarella cheese on one end and roll up the meat, securing the ends with toothpicks.

3. In a large pan, heat the olive oil over medium-high. Add the roll-ups and cook until they are browned on all sides, about 3 minutes per side. Add the onion. Stir to release any browned bits from the bottom of the pan and cook for another 2 minutes, until the onion starts to soften.

4. Add the wine and cook until the alcohol evaporates and the wine is reduced by half, about 4 minutes.

5. Add the tomato juice. Reduce the heat to low, cover the pan, and cook for at least 45 minutes. The beef roll-ups should be very tender when pierced with a fork.

6. Season with salt and pepper to taste. Serve hot.

*Ask your butcher to thinly slice a sirloin roast.

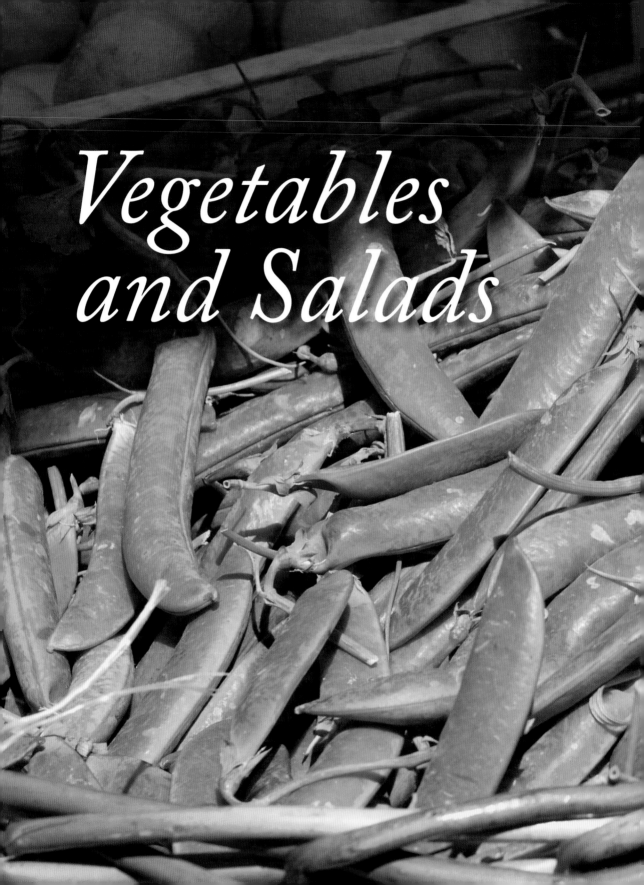

Vegetables and Salads

Vegetables abound in the Puglian diet. Because the region was historically poor and farming was the main occupation of the population, most people grew their own vegetables and invented dozens of ways to prepare them and preserve them for leaner times. To this day, Puglian cooking is mostly vegetable based: vegetables are featured not only in pasta sauces and as accompaniments to meat dishes but also in focaccia and pizza, where they provide texture and nutrients.

Broccoli Raab

Broccoli and broccoli raab (also called rapini) are very common in Puglia. You often see them as side dishes in restaurants or on family dinner tables. Broccoli raab has a strong flavor and a slight bitterness, and it is a perfect complement to many of the pasta dishes in this book—including those with robust meat flavors. As is typical of Puglian dishes, this dish is made more interesting by the addition of red pepper flakes. This is a perfect accompaniment to rich meats, such as sausage or lamb, as well as to simple pasta sauces.

YIELD: 4 SERVINGS

2 tablespoons (30 mL) extra virgin olive oil

2 cloves garlic, peeled and thinly sliced

1 bunch broccoli raab, chopped into bite-sized pieces

1 teaspoon (5 mL) red pepper flakes

Salt, to taste

1. In a large frying pan, heat the oil and garlic over medium-low heat.

2. As soon as the garlic starts to sizzle, increase the heat to medium-high and immediately add the broccoli raab. Toss, season with the red pepper flakes and salt, and cover. Cook for 5 to 6 minutes, until the raab is wilted but not soft.

3. Serve hot.

Green Beans

This simple and quick recipe makes a perfect side dish for many pasta dishes and lighter meats. Getting more vegetables in your diet has never been easier or more flavorful. It is important to use high-quality olive oil, as the flavor of the oil is what makes this dish so uniquely delicious.

Yield: 4 servings

1 pound (454 g) fresh green beans, washed, trimmed, and halved

Salt, to taste

High-quality extra virgin olive oil, for drizzling

1. In a large stock pot, bring 2 quarts (1.9 L) of water to a boil. Add the green beans and cook for 3 minutes, until they start to soften but are still crunchy.

2. Remove the pot from the heat. Drain the beans and immerse them in very cold water to stop the cooking process. Serve with a sprinkle of salt and a drizzle of your favorite extra virgin olive oil.

Green Peppers in Tomato Sauce

Poblano peppers come closest in taste to ripe, green Puglian peppers. This simple yet delicious side dish goes well with simple meat dishes, such as my friend Paola's Chicken with Potatoes (see recipe on page 112). It can also be served with crusty bread, cheese, and olives as part of a vegetarian meal.

(see recipe on page 112).

YIELD: 4 SERVINGS

> 2 tablespoons (30 mL) extra virgin olive oil
>
> 4 poblano peppers, whole
>
> 1 (14-ounce [392-g]) can tomatoes, chopped
>
> Salt, to taste

1. In a medium pan, heat the olive oil over medium-high heat. Add the peppers and cook until they begin to soften. Turn the peppers over halfway through the cooking time, so all sides are cooked equally.

2. When the peppers soften, add the tomatoes and their juice. Cover the pan and cook on medium heat for about 15 minutes.

3. Remove from the heat and transfer to a serving bowl. Season with salt and serve hot or at room temperature.

Roasted Green Peppers

Poblano peppers come closest to the taste of ripe green Puglian peppers. You can use other types of peppers, but avoid green bell peppers, as they do not have the necessary sweetness and flavor. This simple side dish is a perfect complement to any pasta with tomato sauce, including Cavatelli with Beef Roll-Ups (see recipe on page 131) and Cavatelli with Lamb Sauce (see recipe on page 66).

YIELD: 4 SERVINGS

4 poblano peppers

Salt, to taste

High-quality extra virgin olive oil, for drizzling

1. Preheat the broiler to high. Line a baking sheet with foil.

2. Place the peppers on the prepared baking sheet. Roast the peppers under the broiler, turning at least once, for 7 minutes, or until the peppers start to blister. Remove the peppers from the baking sheet, place them in a brown paper bag, and let them cool.

3. When they are cool enough to handle, remove the peppers from the bag. Peel them, sprinkle them with salt, and serve them with a drizzle of olive oil.

Tomato Salad

This simple tomato salad can also be used to make bruschetta. Although not exclusive to Puglia, it is often served on toasted bread as a starter, as it highlights the quality and sweetness of ripe Puglian tomatoes. Try it with the Orecchiette with Broccoli (see recipe on page 74) or the Spaghetti with Zucchini and Pecorino Cheese (see recipe on page 84).

<small>YIELD: 8 SERVINGS</small>

> 1 pound (454 g) ripe tomatoes, chopped
>
> ½ red onion, peeled and finely chopped
>
> 1½ teaspoons (7.5 mL) sea salt
>
> 3 tablespoons (45 mL) extra virgin olive oil
>
> 1½ tablespoons (22.5 mL) red wine vinegar
>
> 1 tablespoon (15 mL) chopped basil

1. In a large bowl, combine the tomatoes and onion. Season with the salt, olive oil, and vinegar.

2. Serve sprinkled with the basil.

Sweet and Sour Peppers

Peppers are very popular in Puglia, and this dish combines some traditional Puglian flavors—the sweetness of the peppers, the added sugar, and the tartness of the vinegar. It is best to use red and yellow bell peppers, because they are sweeter than green bell peppers. This dish makes a great salad to serve with pasta and broccoli or any other pasta dish without tomatoes.

YIELD: 4–6 SERVINGS

3 tablespoons (45 mL) extra virgin olive oil

4 red and yellow bell peppers, cored and cut into strips of equal thickness

1 tablespoon (15 mL) sugar

3 tablespoons (45 mL) white wine vinegar

Salt, to taste

1. In a medium pan, heat the olive oil over medium heat. Add the peppers and cook until they start to soften. Add the sugar and cook for 2 minutes, or until the sugar melts. Add the vinegar and cook for an additional 2 minutes, or until the vinegar evaporates and no longer burns your eyes when you lean over the pan.

2. Transfer to a serving dish and season with salt. Serve warm or at room temperature.

Marinated Zucchini

This is the perfect summer salad—cool, light, and utterly delicious. Use fresh zucchini when it is in season (in the early summer), as it has the most flavor then.

YIELD: 4 SERVINGS

2 medium zucchini, thinly sliced lengthwise

1 tablespoon (15 mL) chopped fresh mint

1 tablespoon (15 mL) extra virgin olive oil

2 tablespoons (30 mL) lemon juice

2 tablespoons (30 mL) pecorino cheese

1. In a mixing bowl, combine all the ingredients. Stir and let sit at room temperature for at least 30 minutes to allow the flavors to combine.

2. Serve chilled or at room temperature.

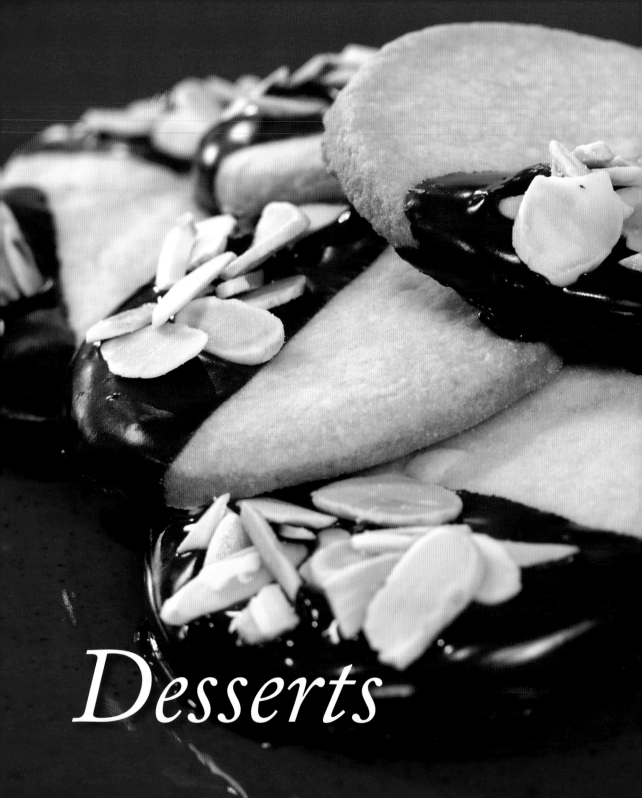

Desserts

In traditional Puglian cuisine, sweets do not appear after every meal—they are usually reserved for holidays and special occasions. Even today, it is more common for people in Puglia to have a piece of fruit after a meal instead of a lavish dessert. However, there are several desserts that are deeply rooted in the region's traditions. These recipes use ingredients grown in Puglia and combine them in interesting and delectable ways.

Shortbread Cookies with Dark Chocolate and Almonds
See recipe on pages 144–145

Shortbread Cookies with Dark Chocolate and Almonds

Dark chocolate and almonds are a common combination in Puglia sweets. These cookies, which are the Italian version of shortbread, are rich and sinfully delicious. Serve them with coffee or after-dinner drinks. It is important to bake the cookies until they turn golden brown, as underbaked shortbread does not have the same flavor. Also, use the highest-quality chocolate you can find for dipping the cookies. The effort is well worth it.

YIELD: 16 SERVINGS

> 2 cups (473 mL) unbleached all-purpose flour, plus more for rolling
>
> ½ cup (118 mL) sugar
>
> ¼ teaspoon (1.25 mL) salt
>
> 7 ounces (196 g) unsalted butter, chilled and cubed
>
> 1 egg
>
> 1 egg yolk
>
> ¾ teaspoon (3.75 mL) pure vanilla extract
>
> 1 teaspoon (5 mL) lemon zest
>
> 8 ounces (227 g) dark chocolate
>
> 4 ounces (112 g) slivered almonds, toasted

1. Preheat the oven to 400°F (200°C).

2. In a clean mixing bowl, combine the flour, sugar, salt, and butter. Mix until the ingredients are combined and the mixture is crumbly.

3. In a separate clean mixing bowl, combine the egg, egg yolk, vanilla extract, and lemon zest, and lightly beat with a fork. Add the egg mixture to the flour mixture and beat with a mixer on low speed for about 2 minutes, or until a dough forms.

4. Turn the dough out onto a lightly floured work surface. Dust your hands with flour and knead the dough for about 1 minute, until it is smooth. Wrap the dough in plastic wrap and chill for at least 1 hour (and up to 4 days). If you chill the dough for longer than 1 hour, let it warm slightly before rolling it out.

5. Roll the dough out on a lightly floured surface. Cut out cookies using a cookie cutter or the rim of a glass.

6. Place the cookies on an ungreased baking sheet and bake for 10 to 12 minutes, or until the edges turn golden brown.

7. Remove the cookies from the baking sheet and cool on a rack for at least 15 minutes.

8. In a double boiler, gently melt the chocolate. When it is completely melted, remove the chocolate from the double boiler, place it in a bowl, and let it cool for 2 minutes.

9. Line a cool baking sheet with foil. Place the slivered almonds in a bowl.

10. Dip half of each cooled cookie in the chocolate. Roll the dipped half of each cookie in the almonds. Place the cookies on the lined the baking sheet to set. Enjoy this bliss alone or with close friends!

Chocolate Tart

This rich and delicious Chocolate Tart (see photo on pages 148–149) is a modern invention in Puglia, where the cuisine has traditionally used locally sourced and more affordable ingredients. This tart is bold and delicious and pairs well with many of the lighter meals in this book. Of course, it can also be served by itself!

YIELD: 8 SERVINGS

For the pastry:

2 cups (473 mL) unbleached all-purpose flour, plus more for rolling

½ cup (118 mL) sugar

¼ teaspoon (1.25 mL) salt

7 ounces (196 g) unsalted butter

1 egg

1 egg yolk

¾ teaspoon (3.75 mL) pure vanilla extract

1 teaspoon (5 mL) lemon zest

For the filling:

1¾ ounces (49 g) all-purpose flour

1¾ ounces (49 g) dark cocoa

3½ ounces (98 g) sugar

2 cups (473 mL) milk

2 teaspoons (10 mL) orange zest

1. Make the pastry. In a clean mixing bowl, combine the flour, sugar, salt, and butter. Mix until the ingredients are combined and the mixture is crumbly.

2. In a separate clean mixing bowl, combine the egg, egg yolk, vanilla extract, and lemon zest, and lightly beat with a fork. Add the egg mixture to the flour mixture and beat with a mixer on low speed for about 2 minutes, until a dough forms.

3. Turn the dough out onto a lightly floured work surface. Dust your hands with flour and knead the dough for about 1 minute, until it is smooth. Wrap the dough in plastic wrap and chill for at least 1 hour (or up to 4 days). If you chill the dough for longer than 1 hour, let it warm slightly before rolling it out.

4. Grease a tart dish. Roll the dough out on a lightly floured surface to a thickness of ¼ inch (0.5 cm) and place it in the prepared dish. Trim the excess dough off the edges.

5. Preheat the oven to 400°F (200°C).

6. Make the filling. In a saucepan, combine the flour, cocoa, and sugar and stir until thoroughly mixed.

7. In a separate saucepan, warm the milk over medium heat, but do not let it boil.

8. Remove the milk from the heat and slowly add it to the flour mixture, whisking to break up any lumps. Bring the milk–flour mixture to a boil over medium heat, stirring constantly, until the mixture forms a custard-like consistency.

9. Remove the filling from the heat and transfer it to a clean mixing bowl. Add the orange zest and let it cool.

10. Spread the cool chocolate filling into the tart shell. Bake for 30 minutes.

Chocolate Tart · **PAGES 146–147**

Jam Tart

Tarts with a variety of jams and fruit preserves are one of the most common Puglian desserts. Puglia grows a lot of fruit, and much of it is preserved in jams and marmalades. These home-made preserves are then used to make tarts of all sorts. Use high-quality jam or preserves (figs, which are pictured at right, and apricots work well), as they really shine in this dish.

YIELD: 8 SERVINGS

2 cups (473 mL) unbleached all-purpose flour, plus more for rolling

½ cups (118 mL) sugar

¼ teaspoon (1.25 mL) salt

7 ounces (196 g) unsalted butter

1 egg

1 egg yolk

¾ teaspoon (3.75 mL) pure vanilla extract

1 teaspoon (5 mL) lemon zest

1½ cups (354 mL) marmalade of your choice

½ cup (118 mL) slivered almonds

1. In a clean mixing bowl, combine the flour, sugar, salt, and butter. Mix until the ingredients are combined and the mixture is crumbly.

2. In a separate clean mixing bowl, combine the egg, egg yolk, vanilla extract, and lemon zest, and lightly beat with a fork. Add the egg mixture to the flour mixture and beat with a mixer on low speed for about 2 minutes, or until a dough forms.

3. Turn the dough out onto a lightly floured work surface. Dust your hands with flour and knead the dough for about 1 minute, or until it is smooth. Wrap the dough in plastic wrap and chill for at least 1 hour (or up to 4 days). If you chill the dough for longer than 1 hour, let it warm slightly before rolling it out.

4. Grease a tart dish. Roll the dough out on a lightly floured surface to a thickness of ¼ inch (0.5 cm) and place it in the prepared dish. Trim the excess dough off the edges and roll it into a ball. Roll the ball of leftover dough out to a thickness of ¼ inch (0.5 cm) and cut into strips.

5. Preheat the oven to 400°F (200°C).

6. Spread the marmalade in the tart dish. Sprinkle it with the almonds and cover with a lattice of the dough strips.

7. Bake for 35 minutes.

Apple Tart

My friend Paola shared this recipe with me by during an all-day cooking session in Ostuni. A lighter version of American apple pie, it works well as a midafternoon snack or a dessert after a light lunch or dinner.

Yield: 8 servings

2 cups (473 mL) unbleached all-purpose flour, plus more for rolling

½ cup (118 mL) sugar

¼ teaspoon (1.25 mL) salt

7 ounces (196 g) unsalted butter

1 egg

1 egg yolk

¾ teaspoon (3.75 mL) pure vanilla extract

1 teaspoon (5 mL) lemon zest

3 Golden Delicious apples, peeled, cored, and sliced

3 tablespoons (45 mL) brown sugar

3 tablespoons (45 mL) lemon juice

1. In a clean mixing bowl, combine the flour, sugar, salt, and butter. Mix until the ingredients are combined and the mixture is crumbly.

2. In a separate clean mixing bowl, combine the egg, egg yolk, vanilla extract, and lemon zest, and lightly beat with a fork. Add the egg mixture to the flour mixture and beat with a mixer on low speed for about 2 minutes, or until a dough forms.

3. Turn the dough out onto a lightly floured work surface. Dust your hands with flour and knead the dough for about 1 minute, until it is smooth. Wrap the dough in plastic wrap and chill for at least 1 hour (or up to 4 days). If you chill the dough for longer than 1 hour, let it warm slightly before rolling it out.

4. Grease a tart dish. Roll the dough out on a lightly floured surface to a thickness of ¼ inch (0.5 cm) and place it in the prepared dish. Trim the excess dough off the edges and roll it into a ball. Roll the ball of leftover dough out to a thickness of ¼ inch (0.5 cm) and cut it into strips.

5. Preheat the oven to 400°F (200°C).

6. Arrange the apples in the tart dish. Sprinkle the apples with the brown sugar and lemon juice, and cover with a lattice of the dough strips.

7. Bake for at least 35 minutes, or until the tart is golden brown on top.

Coffee Pudding

This light dessert is easy to make and has lots of flavor. It is the perfect ending to any meal, and even guests who do not drink coffee enjoy its delicate flavor and smooth texture. The pudding can also be made ahead, which makes preparing a full dinner much less stressful.

Yield: 8 servings

> 2 cups (473 mL) milk
>
> 2 eggs
>
> 4 egg yolks
>
> ¾ cup (177 mL) sugar
>
> ½ cup (118 mL) espresso or very strong coffee, cooled

1. Preheat the oven to 400°F (200°C).

2. In a saucepan, warm the milk over medium-low heat, but do not let it boil.

3. In a clean mixing bowl, combine the eggs, egg yolks, and sugar and beat on high speed for 5 to 6 minutes, or until the mixture is thick and light colored. Add the coffee to the mixture.

4. Temper the warmed milk into the mixture, a little bit at a time, stirring constantly as you go to prevent the eggs from scrambling.

5. Grease 8 individual ramekins. When all the ingredients are combined and the mixture has a uniform texture, divide it among the prepared ramekins.

6. Place the ramekins in a large baking dish. Pour water around the ramekins in the dish until it reaches halfway up the sides of the ramekins.

7. Bake for about 40 minutes, or until the pudding in the ramekins is almost set. The pudding will continue to set as it cools, so do not bake until firm or it will be too dry.

8. Cool to room temperature and then refrigerate for up to 2 days. Serve cold.

Index

About the Author

VIKTORIJA TODOROVSKA IS A FOOD AND WINE EDUCATOR WITH A PASSION FOR exploring the world of food through simple and flavorful combinations of high-quality ingredients. She studied Italian cooking at Apicius, the International School of Hospitality in Florence. Since her first visit to the southern Italian region of Puglia, she has been fascinated by its foods, wines, and people. She lives in Chicago, where she teaches cooking and wine courses. Her website is www.olivacooking.com.